"For all of those who've been s[...] unlock the greatness that is insi[...] In his book *Mantled for Greatness*, Joshua Giles skillfully and prophetically walks you through the process of transformation and transition required to equip you to handle the mantle!"

Isaac Pitre, president of Isaac Pitre Ministries, leader of II Kings Global Network, isaacpitre.org

"As usual, another revelatory book from Prophet Giles that had me reading nonstop and gave me clarity about my own mantle for deliverance. A must-read for all Kingdom people who have been called for specialized ministry in the Body of Christ."

Apostle Alexander Pagani, bestselling author of *The Secrets to Deliverance*

"In his book *Mantled for Greatness*, Joshua Giles brilliantly leads you from the beginning seeds of faith to the manifestation of God's greatness within you. As you read, your ceiling will become your floor. You will be mantled for your God-given assignment and empowered to become a vessel of God's glory. Everything you've walked through has prepared you for such a time as this."

Matt Sorger, prophetic minister, spiritual mentor, transformational health coach

"*Mantled for Greatness* is a book about the action of faith and the process of moving from *small* to *greatness*. What really spoke to me was how we are the innovative solutions to big problems. Joshua Giles shows us that when we examine and channel our abilities through the Spirit of God, we can multiply in incredible ways. You have the capacity to be great! This book will help you unlock the well of greatness within you. Once unlocked, your greatness can be transferred to another generation!"

Dr. Chuck D. Pierce, president of Glory of Zion International and Kingdom Harvest Alliance

MANTLED
FOR
GREATNESS

MANTLED
FOR
GREATNESS

YOUR PROPHETIC GUIDE TO RELEASING
A GOD-SIZED DREAM

JOSHUA GILES

Chosen

a division of Baker Publishing Group
Minneapolis, Minnesota

© 2023 by Joshua Thomas Giles

Published by Chosen Books
Minneapolis, Minnesota
www.chosenbooks.com

Chosen Books is a division of
Baker Publishing Group, Grand Rapids, Michigan

Printed in the United States of America

Library of Congress Cataloging-in-Publication Data
Names: Giles, Joshua, author.
Title: Mantled for greatness : your prophetic guide to releasing a God-sized dream / Joshua Giles.
Description: Minneapolis, Minnesota : Chosen Books, a division of Baker Publishing Group, [2023] | Includes bibliographical references.
Identifiers: LCCN 2023014031 | ISBN 9780800762391 (trade paper) | ISBN 9780800763688 (casebound) | ISBN 9781493445387 (ebook)
Subjects: LCSH: Self-realization—Religious aspects—Christianity. | Self-acceptance—Religious aspects—Christianity.
Classification: LCC BV4647.S43 G56 2023 | DDC 248.4—dc23/eng/20230818
LC record available at https://lccn.loc.gov/2023014031

Author is represented by the literary agency of Embolden Media Group Agency.

Baker Publishing Group publications use paper produced from sustainable forestry practices and post-consumer waste whenever possible.

23   24   25   26   27   28   29   8   7   6   5   4   3   2

I would like to take the time to dedicate this book
to the amazing members of the organizations that I've had
the honor of founding, the Mantle Network and Joshua
Giles Ministries. Mantle Network pastors and leaders and
JGM partners, you are an extraordinary family of believers
and the best tribe I could ask for. I love and honor you.
This is your season to walk in the greatness of your mantle
and see the promises of God manifested in your life.

CONTENTS

FOREWORD

Greatness is a concept that has captivated and inspired human beings throughout history. We study the lives of individuals because somewhere deep inside, we know the potential for greatness lies within us, too. It is a state of being that we strive to achieve, a pinnacle of achievement that many of us aspire to reach because it is a part of our divine destiny. Scriptures declare, "He who is in you is greater than he who is in the world." Unfortunately, for many, that's where their greatness will remain—buried within. But what exactly is greatness? Do fame and fortune define it, or is it something more profound?

Joshua Giles explores the concept of greatness from various angles and perspectives. He's a prophetic giant in his own right, and this book unravels the prophetic dimensions of greatness. You will delve into the lives of individuals who have achieved greatness in their respective fields. Take a deep dive to unearth the traits and characteristics commonly associated with greatness, such as perseverance, passion, and a willingness to take risks. Explore the societal factors contributing to creating and recognizing greatness, from cultural norms to economic systems. Learn about the ways of God, who makes greatness accessible to us all.

Greatness is a spiritual heritage. This brilliant author provides insights and inspiration for anyone striving to achieve greatness in their own life. Whether you are an aspiring entrepreneur, an up-and-coming creative, or someone who wants to impact the world positively, the stories and lessons in these pages will be valuable to you. They show those who influence the corporate trajectories of companies, communities, and countries.

At the heart of this fascination with these influencers lies the concept of mantles—the unseen force behind greatness. In a world increasingly focused on the material and tangible, it is easy to forget the importance of our life's intangible, unseen, and spiritual aspects. The realm of the spirit is a crucial component of our existence, and understanding it can provide us with a more profound sense of purpose, meaning, and fulfillment.

Prophet Giles has taken on the crucial task of exploring this fascinating and often mysterious realm. Drawing on a range of spiritual traditions and teachings, practical and personal anecdotes, testimonies, and stories, he presents a comprehensive guide to the world of the spirit, providing insights and practical advice on how to navigate this realm and harness its power to succeed, progress, and prosper in our modern world as God's representative.

This book is a journey into the human experience of seeking knowledge and understanding about the future. From exploring the nature of the soul to delving into the workings and wonders of God, this book covers a wide range of topics that will inspire and enlighten you. Whether you are a spiritual seeker or simply curious about the nature of God, the prophetic, or the mysterious nature of mantles, this book will be an invaluable resource for those serious about being used by God.

With its clear, accessible, and readable style, this book, a true tour de force, will surely become a classic in the prophetic field.

Whether you are a seasoned student of prophecy, a skeptic, a believer, a student of history, or a curious reader, I invite you to join the myriads of individuals on this journey who have enjoyed preceding installments on this intriguing topic by an author who himself has been recognized as one of the leading contemporary prophets in this generation. This book offers a rich and thought-provoking exploration of one of the most enduring and enigmatic aspects of human experience—the achievement of greatness.

Greatness comes in many forms. It can be found in the bold vision of an entrepreneur who disrupts industries and changes lives. It shines through the perseverance of an athlete who pushes their body and mind beyond perceived limits to achieve remarkable feats. It echoes in the artistic expression of a musician, a preacher, a psalmist, a teacher, an emancipator, or a painter who moves hearts and leaves a lasting imprint on the world. But greatness also manifests in the quiet acts of compassion, volunteerism, and service to humanity, in the teachers who ignite the flames of knowledge in their students, mothers, and fathers, and in the everyday heroes who make a difference in the lives of others.

In a world full of dreams and aspirations, greatness is a beacon that guides us, inspiring us to go beyond our limits and reach for the extraordinary. Greatness is not a destination but a journey—a path paved with dedication, resilience, and an unwavering belief in our potential.

I am honored to have been allowed to write this foreword and highly recommend this book to anyone seeking to deepen their understanding of the spiritual realm. Join the author on this journey as he seeks to give you a greater understanding of the elusive concept of greatness and what it truly means to be great.

As you immerse yourself in the chapters ahead, let these words be a guiding light that illuminates your path toward greatness. Embrace the biblical wisdom shared within these pages, for it can transform your mindset, ignite your passion, and embolden your quest for excellence as you pursue your God-given purpose and life mission.

Dr. N. Cindy Trimm, author, global thought leader,
servant of God

ACKNOWLEDGMENTS

I would like to acknowledge some valuable people who God sent into my life and who have helped to support the prophetic message that fills the pages of this book. To the late Scott Holtz: Your passion, tenacity, and push affected me deeply. The anointing that he carried on the earth is still felt today by those who knew him. Thank you for being my friend and a mighty warrior in the Lord. You are truly missed.

To my literary agent, Jevon Bolden, thank you for taking a chance on me. When others didn't see the writing gift and passion for being a prophetic scribe in me, you did. Partnering with you to release powerful, prophetic content has been an exhilarating journey! To my acquisitions editor and the editorial director of Chosen books, Kim Bangs: You've been such a gift that God has placed in my life to help incubate compelling material that reaches the world with the message of Jesus. You'll never know just how much it means to me to know how you spoke up for my first manuscript when it came across your desk, when many didn't know who I was. I appreciate you!

Lastly, thank you to my parents and my family (they're way too many to name) and especially my brothers. We grew up experiencing the hardships of life not fully understanding that God placed seeds of greatness within us. It's taken me years to realize just how blessed we were, even when it didn't look like it. God used every challenge and struggle to develop His greatness on the inside of us. May you continue to walk in the fullness of who God has called you to be. I love you all.

1

SMALL IS THE NEW BIG

The steps of a good man are ordered by the LORD, and He
delights in his way.

Psalm 37:23

I dropped my luggage at check-in and ran as fast as I could. I
was racing through the quaint, but at the time newly expanded,
Raleigh-Durham airport. It felt as if I were running a marathon
to catch my flight. With just two suitcases and very little money
in my bank account, I was leaving everything that I knew and
had become familiar with to chase after a vision that I believe
God had placed in my heart. I only really knew a handful of
people in the new city I was moving to, and I was going to need
faith to traverse this new terrain ahead of me. I had this sense
that I was carrying something that was going to make a big
impact on the people I was called to minister to.

When I arrived in Minnesota, I quickly made it to the little
apartment I had rented. It was completely empty. As I talked on
the phone or prayed aloud, I could hear my voice bouncing off

the walls, reaching a crescendo that mimicked being in an auditorium. But it was just an empty apartment. I thought, *God, how am I going to manage pastoring a new church plant, paying for new facilities, and covering my own personal expenses?* I realized that I had stepped into uncharted waters that could only be mastered by faith.

What I've come to learn is that when you have a vision and faith in God, He will always take you beyond your abilities, beyond your understanding, and far beyond the money you have. It's only when you come to the end of yourself that you can fully walk in the manifestation of God's vision for your life. You must become comfortable with being uncomfortable. Any divine assignment, major project, or mission that God gives always come with pressure, difficulty, and uncomfortableness. When you feel those things, it's often an indicator that you're on the right track. In my experience, God uses trials, tests, and pressure to reveal what's really in a person. *Sometimes the storm you're in is really a simulation to unlock your greatest potential.*

In the book of Ezekiel, the Spirit of God takes Ezekiel into a series of visions or supernatural encounters. In chapter 47, He brings Ezekiel into the inner court or the door of the Temple. Mysteriously, a small trickle of water begins to seep under the threshold of the door from the south side. In this vision, there was an angel or man with Ezekiel, measuring the length and breadth of the Temple:

> Going on eastward with a measuring line in his hand, the man measured a thousand cubits, and then led me through the water, and it was ankle-deep. Again he measured a thousand, and led me through the water, and it was knee-deep. Again he measured a thousand, and led me through the water, and it was waist-deep.
>
> Ezekiel 47:3–4 ESV

What started off small soon became a mighty river. In Scripture, this water represents life, renewal, and that which is needed to fuel and sustain life. Water here is also symbolic of the Holy Spirit. The significant part of this passage is that the water started off small. Many people underestimate the small things in their lives, because to some people, small means insignificant. But that's not the case. Whenever God creates something, He always starts it in seed form. He never gives us the finished product first. It's easy to overlook the small seed because it doesn't physically show that it will become a great tree, producing much fruit. Yet God is moving in the small things. *In this season, the things that seem insignificant and that don't seem big will have big impact. That's the new strategy from heaven. God is placing impactful things into small packages.*

In the interactive vision Ezekiel had, as the angel took him through the Temple, the water started at his ankles. The ankle is the joint that connects the leg and foot. It is the connector that moves the foot. God showed Ezekiel imagery of the stages that every vision or assignment must move through. Your feet are symbolic of the path you take; they represent your direction, purpose, and destiny. When you're moving into uncharted waters, being led by the Holy Spirit, your feet have to be submerged in the water first. Your direction and steps must be completely ordered by Him. This comes through righteousness or living upright before the Lord (see Psalm 37:23).

Next, Ezekiel moved knee-deep. The knees are the largest joints in the body. They either allow a person to stand upright or kneel. Kneeling is an act of submission, worship, and yielding. When you, along with your vision, move into knee-deep waters, it's a sign that you are breaking pride and humbling yourself under the mighty hand of God.

What started off as just a trickle of water began to swell to the point that soon Ezekiel was waist-deep in the river that was now flowing. This means that he was semi-submerged in the water. When you are partially submerged in the glory of the Lord, you can feel the current, but you are still somewhat in control. Eventually, the water got to the point where it was out of Ezekiel's control. It was deep enough to swim in. Ezekiel 47:5 (ESV) says,

> Again he measured a thousand, and it was a river that I could not pass through, for the water had risen. It was deep enough to swim in, a river that could not be passed through.

Each time the angel measured, the water grew. I believe firmly that there are angels assigned to help you measure the expanse of your assignment and spiritual territory. Each time you take a step, they measure. And each time they measure, the water level rises, until you are submerged in the glory of God. This great vision shown to Ezekiel started from just a few small drops of water and then exploded into something "mega." This will also be true for you. What starts small in your life will become mega. Mega comes from the Greek word *megas*.[1] It's the word *greater*. It's referenced in John 14:12, when Jesus says of each one who believes in Him, "Greater works than these he will do." I believe that God is mantling individuals to carry "greater."

Small Churches, Small Groups, Family Units

In our small storefront church, we could barely fit sixty chairs in the place we had carved out as the sanctuary. We had done all the work ourselves by taking this little warehouse area and laying carpet, painting walls, and fixing it up as best we could. I remember staying up all night painting walls. I woke up the next morning aching in places I didn't even know I could ache in. In this small building, we had some of the most electrifying services. We saw some of the greatest miracles and conversions. The Shekinah glory of God would be so thick during our services that sometimes we would see smoke or a haze in the sanctuary. The presence of God was tangible. The all-night prayer services were explosive. We would pray with such force that it felt as if the walls were shaking. We would see God answer those prayers, and pure, heartfelt praises to God would erupt. These experiences would sometimes last for hours as we lost track of time because the encounters were just that good. On one occasion, just a handful of us were there praying when I heard God say, *I'm sending you to the nations.*

I thought to myself, *Our church is so small; it's just a few of us. How are we going to go to the nations from a storefront church?*

It was at that moment that the Holy Spirit was teaching me about faith. God was teaching me that the impact of your reach is not predicated on the size of your ministry. He was showing me that He would defy the odds and human logic and raise up a global ministry from what some would have considered a hole-in-the-wall building. This is a lesson you must also understand. The size of your building, ministry, and finances is not what's important. The size of your faith is what really matters.

As I prayed that day in my church, the Holy Spirit spoke the name of a specific European country to me. A holy boldness rose up in me as I began to declare the name of this country out loud. God was telling me to speak boldly, in a command tone, that we would go to this country. With authority, I was declaring that any opposition would be removed.

Shortly after this, someone called the church office randomly from this same country, with an invitation to minister there. I answered the phone and spoke with this person, who was a pastor. I was in shock that God had moved so quickly. I asked, "How did you find out about this ministry?"

The pastor replied, "I don't really know. Somehow God led me to you."

This was the start of ministry in the nations. It all started from a storefront church where God supernaturally opened doors and brought us opportunities for missions and international ministry.

I believe that over the next several years we will see God highlight small ministries, churches, and families that will spark awakenings, stir up revivals, and be the driving force for the move of God in the earth. According to a *Lifeway Research* study, congregations in the United States are increasingly small. Nearly 70 percent of churches in America are under 100 people.[2] According to *Christianity Today*, 90 percent of churches have under 200 people.[3] That makes up the great majority of churches in this country. Some people take a negative approach to interpreting this data. They say that the Church is declining. I say that the Church is morphing into a book of Acts model. Thousands came to Christ through the powerful evangelistic efforts of the apostles. The Church wasn't labeled by a building or specific ministry gift back then; its people were called the Church in a particular city—the Church in Thyatira or the Church in Philadelphia. All believers in that city or region made up the Church. Yes, they gathered in the synagogues. However, they also had small gatherings in houses and little communities. They did life together:

> So continuing daily with one accord in the temple, and breaking bread from house to house, they ate their food with gladness and simplicity of heart (Acts 2:46).

> And daily in the temple, and in every house, they did not cease teaching and preaching Jesus as the Christ (Acts 5:42).

> . . . how I kept back nothing that was helpful, but proclaimed it to you, and taught you publicly and from house to house (Acts 20:20).

The expansion of Christianity and the Church happened organically. It wasn't in the big or large happenings. The secret to the expansion was through small house-to-house fellowship. Small house churches, gathering in the marketplace and on street corners, with ordinary people passionate about an extraordinary God. The same kind of expansion will happen in our day through small churches, small groups, and family units. Let's explore each of these areas where we can do life together.

Small Churches

In the coming days, small churches will dominate and help drive the next move of God. Signs, wonders, and miracles will be seen confirming the Gospel that is preached. Emphasis will be placed on community and fellowship.

Because of the difficult years and times of tragedy the world has seen, mental health and wholeness will also be a focus. These thriving, yet intimate churches will be houses of prayer and healing that will help nurse people back to spiritual health.

Large churches will always be there; they are needed and impact culture in a unique way. But the new mega-churches are small churches. People will begin to search out these small gatherings because of their ability to focus on individuals in a personal and loving way. Small ministries have been the bedrock of communities since the inception of my nation and many others, and they will continue to thrive.

Small Groups

These are gatherings of around ten to twelve people, or even fewer. Small groups are a collection of brothers and sisters in Christ coming together to encourage one another in the Word, eat together, fellowship together, and simply do life with one another. One of the major tactics of the enemy is isolation, which is one of the ways Satan tries to take advantage of believers.

When we are isolated for too long, we can become weakened in our faith and opened to unnecessary attacks. Christ's Body is designed for us to be fitly joined together, with many members making up one Body. We were made to draw strength from fellowship and community.

The Holy Spirit showed me that we will see a rise of small groups again. Isaiah 65:8 reveals that new wine is found in the cluster of grapes. New wine is symbolic of the Holy Spirit's outpouring and anointing. His outpouring is found in people coming together with one mind and one spirit, in the unity of the faith. The next awakening will be fueled by small groups that are on fire for God. Evangelism will be a key focus of these groups that reach out into their communities. Some groups will form strategically within churches, while others will form organically from friends who are brothers and sisters in Christ.

Some people have fought the idea of small groups, thinking they are unneeded or outdated. This is the furthest thing from the truth. Do you know who formed the first small group in the New Testament? Jesus! Yes, that's right—Jesus gathered twelve men (see Matthew 10:1–4). Some were fishermen, some businessmen, one was a political zealot, and one was even a tax collector. This was a small group of disciples, who became apostles (sent ones), who turned the world upside down through the message of the Gospel.

Family Units

Families are the core groups that make up the foundation for everything in our world. Most immediate family units are small in comparison to other, larger groups. The average family unit is three or four people in the United States.[4] Families are God's building blocks for the Church. Before God created and instituted the Church, He created the family unit. Adam and Eve weren't placed in a city; they were placed in a garden. They were fruitful and started a family. This is a prophetic picture of what the family unit has been designed to do. Families are called to plant, water, and manage gardens spiritually. Parents plant words, love, and care into their children, and by doing so, they reap a harvest. The most valuable and irreplaceable collection of people groups is the family unit. For this reason, we have seen the enemy step up his attacks against families all over the world.

You don't have to look far to see families broken, torn apart, or hurting. But we are about to see that change. A wave of family restoration and revival is coming! I believe we are about to see families coming back together. Many generational wounds will be healed, and fragmented family units will be restored. When the family unit is restored, neighborhoods will be revitalized. When the family unit is restored, crime rates in cities will drop. When the family unit is restored, schools will be overrun with prayer and testimonies of the goodness of God. Family is the one entity that intersects with every single facet of society. When God wants to release a move of His Spirit, I believe He desires to use the vehicle of family because it has the ability to influence every system.

In Scripture, the Lord called Gideon and handpicked him from his father's house. God told him that he would deliver the children of Israel out of the hands of their enemies, the Midianites. Gideon was anointed by God as a mighty warrior and man of valor. In answering the call of God, he makes a reference to his family:

> Then the LORD turned to him and said, "Go in this might of yours, and you shall save Israel from the hand of the Midianites. Have I not sent you?"
>
> So he said to Him, "O my LORD, how can I save Israel? Indeed my clan is the weakest in Manasseh, and I am the least in my father's house."
>
> Judges 6:14–15

Gideon referred to his family as being poor. They didn't have much status in Israel. They didn't have substance or much in terms of material possessions. Because of this, he felt as though he wasn't worthy or possibly wasn't even capable of being a prophetic deliverer for Israel. Yet God used Gideon to become a mighty deliverer and to lead Israel in victory, defeating the Midianites. From this we can learn that it's not about your family's status. Like Gideon, your family may be poor. Your family members may not have gone to the best schools or have the most glamorous jobs. But what you do have is the hand of the Lord on your family. And that's all you need. Out of small family units, God will raise up deliverers, creators, innovators, and revolutionary thinkers to shift the culture and bring Christ's message of hope.

Small Businesses and the Rise of Entrepreneurs

Small is the new big will not just be the mantra for the Church; it will also spread throughout society and into the business world. For many decades, large conglomerates and huge companies have had somewhat of a monopoly on their industries. This is changing now, and you get to be part of it. Small businesses and small business owners will rise and dominate their industries once again. Small businesses are the backbone of any thriving economy in a capitalist society. I believe there is a special anointing coming on business owners to serve others well and experience increase at the same time.

If you're an aspiring entrepreneur or are thinking about starting a business, if God has placed such an idea in you, now just may be the time for you to start it. Start with what you have, and use what's in your wheelhouse. Sometimes we think we must have this genius, grand idea that wows everyone. It's easy to overthink an idea. I've found that the greatest blessings are hidden in the simplest ideas. Sometimes it's the small things that make the biggest impact.

Over the years, I have taught many business seminars and workshops. When I polled the attendees, I found that people have a hard time in the beginning phases of a business. They can often become discouraged when they don't see big sales numbers, or when they have just a few customers. Sometimes people fail to realize that starting a thing is half the battle.

Zechariah 4:10 (NLT) says, "Do not despise these small beginnings, for the LORD rejoices to see the work begin." Do not hate or despise the small beginnings in your life. If you have a vision, a dream, a ministry, an assignment, or an initiative, don't overlook it just because it might be small. Small can be mega when God breathes on it. Here are several points to help you realize that although what you have may seem small, you're carrying something mega:

- *Small can be a strategy to preserve you over the long haul.* Sometimes when something is physically big, there's more of a target placed on it. God will hide mega vision in small packages so you can avoid unnecessary warfare.
- *It's not about the size of the crowd; God looks at the size of your faith.* God isn't interested in who's following you or who likes what you're doing. He is more interested in knowing that you are following Him against all odds. When you carry mega faith, you can move the most impossible mountains.
- *Everything that God created began in seed form.* A seed, although small, has the potential to become a great oak tree. It's not just magnificent when it's standing tall as a massive tree. It's glorious and miraculous to know that all of that came from a small seed. When you realize that God gives the greatest visions in seed form (thoughts, ideas, impressions on the heart), you'll value them as treasures and nurture them to see them grow.

- *Just because it looks big doesn't always mean it's growth; when something is infected, it swells also.* Healthy growth is seen by its solid foundation and its fruit. Just because something looks big doesn't mean it's healthy. Don't chase after looking big. Pursue being spiritually, emotionally, mentally, and physically healthy.

MANTLE MOMENT

The mantle the Lord is placing upon your life is like an incubator. It has the ability to take a small dream and develop it into something great. In order to fully access the small seeds God has placed within you to impact the world around you, I want you to do this quick exercise. Write down a few *small dreams* that you've left unattended. Then take a little time to pray concerning these dreams. Afterward, circle one or two to focus on as you read this book. You can refer back to this list as you read and complete the other *Mantle Moment* exercises at the end of each chapter, building on what you have started here.

2

YOU, THE BIG IDEA!

I praise you, for I am fearfully and wonderfully made. Wonderful are your works; my soul knows it very well.

Psalm 139:14 ESV

Lucifer was once described as one of the most beautiful of God's creations. He was covered in the most precious and stunning stones, including sardius, topaz, and diamond. He was ladened with beryl, onyx, and jasper, with splendid sapphire, turquoise, and emerald with gold (see Ezekiel 28:13–14). The Bible describes him as fashioned with timbrels, which are percussion instruments resembling either a drum or tambourine. In addition, he had pipes that were created within him, and stringed instruments that accompanied him (see Isaiah 14:11–12). He was once a beautiful, musical masterpiece—until the day that iniquity was found in him.

Lucifer was the only angel described as anointed in the Bible. He was the anointed cherub that Scripture reveals was in the

Garden of Eden. God created Adam and Eve and placed them in the Garden, too. Some speculate that Lucifer's iniquity led him to become jealous. It's highly probable that he was there in the Garden before Adam and Eve. Then he sees this new creation being given dominion over a place that he has dwelt in. Who were these human creations, made from the dust of the earth? They had no drums, symbols, pipes, or violins built within them. No beautiful jewels or diamonds covered them. Just dust fashioned into bones, skin, ligaments, and tendons, with the breath of God flowing through their lungs. As the author of Psalm 8 asks, "What is man that You are mindful of him, and the son of man that You visit him?" (verse 4).

Although humankind didn't have the glorious, extravagant beauty other creations may have had, God placed a treasure hidden deep inside the human spirit. You see, God made us in His image and likeness. He made humankind as speaking spirits with the ability to create and declare, just as He does. Lucifer's jealousy led him to try to trick Adam and Eve out of their inheritance and true divine purpose. Although they sinned, grace came in the form of a man who was God in the flesh, Jesus Christ.

I believe that Lucifer couldn't understand why God gave humanity the one thing that he didn't have. When you study the human body, you'll find that the diaphragm and esophagus are in the shape of a shofar. The one instrument that God gave humanity is a horn—a trumpet. We have the ability to release God's voice and sound in the earth. Isn't that amazing?!

Not only that, but God entrusted humanity to carry His Kingdom. Hidden in the most unassuming clay vessels, He placed His Kingdom, rulership, authority, and dominion. "Now we have this treasure in clay jars, so that this extraordinary power may be from God and not from us," says 2 Corinthians 4:7 (CSB). Luke 17:21 confirms that "indeed, the kingdom of God is within you."

Let's take a closer look at Psalm 8 as well. Verse 5 adds of mankind, "For You have made him a little lower than the angels, and You have crowned him with glory and honor." This seems to state that God made humanity a little lower than the angels. I've heard this taught and quoted for years. When I was pursuing my master's degree in theological studies years ago, one of the things I learned was to look deeper into the translation of words. We took a class that delved into the mistranslation of words from Scripture into our English language. Psalm 8:5 contains one of those examples. The word *angels* is a mistranslation. The actual Hebrew word there is *elohiym*, which means creator, or the supreme God, or the God of Israel.[1] This Scripture verse is really conveying to us that God made human beings a little lower than Himself.

When God created the heavens and earth, He had you in mind. When He fashioned the firmament, stars, land, and seas, He had you in mind. When He put the foundations of the earth in place, He was thinking of you. That's right! You are God's big idea for stewarding the earth, bringing solutions to earthly problems, giving praises and glory back to Him, and walking in divine authority.

You Are the Answer to Prayer

A mentor of mine had given me a prophetic word that I'd be called to a certain European city. The prophecy was so detailed that it was alarming. This prophet said, "You're going to meet a man on a train 10 kilometers north [from your point of entry]. This man will take you into the city, and you will find favor in this European city. There's going to be a move of God there as you minister."

The prophecy continued, describing the power of God that would come upon my team and me. I could feel the presence of God strongly as I received this prophetic word. As a couple of years passed, I soon forgot this prophecy, although I had recorded it. Then I got a call from a stranger whom I had encountered in a service, whom the Holy Spirit had led me to pray for. I had no idea that he would become a gateway for me into several countries for ministry.

Just as the prophecy had indicated, I was invited to a European city, which happened to be Frankfurt, Germany, and eventually to a small town in the countryside. I would go to multiple cities in Europe on this same trip, but when I first arrived, I met this same man on a train. We traveled quite a distance before arriving at the hotel. The name of the hotel struck me: *Favored Plaza Hotel*. Again, the prophetic word came back to me: "You will find favor in this European city." I thought to myself, *This is a sign.*

Truly, there was such favor with the churches there. I ministered at a church where the people were so open and hungry for the Word that revival began to break out. Healings began to manifest all over as people with conditions were called out by supernatural knowledge, and the Lord healed them instantly. It was amazing to witness. My team and I cried because we were so touched by how God was moving. At the end of the service, I prayed for the pastor. I could see fatigue and the years of labor taking a toll. This pastor began to shake under the presence of God as the glory of the Lord manifested in a strong way. I gave a detailed prophetic word and closed the service. After the event was over, the pastor was flooded with joy and tears. The testimony came pouring out. Although this was years ago, his words have stuck with me till this day. "I've been praying for a move of God like this for fifteen years!" the pastor exclaimed. "God sent you as an answer to my prayer."

At that moment, I became acutely aware that God has designed people as answers to prayer. *You carry the solution, the clarity, the encouragement, and maybe even the demonstrative power of God that someone has been earnestly praying for.*

When you realize that you are a word from God, your entire paradigm will shift. You came out of the mouth of God; He breathed you into existence. And His word cannot return to Him void or incomplete. Further, this means that you are called to invade and occupy a world that is in need of a word or answer from God.

You Are the Solution

A solution is a particular instance or method of solving a challenge or problem. God has strategically made you to be a problem solver. This function can only be activated, according to James 1:5, by asking God for His wisdom. The wisdom of God is the influence, intelligence, and insight of the Holy Spirit on the human mind or psyche. Through this divine force, you can wield knowledge, revelation, and skills to resolve issues and challenges that people face today. Being the solution doesn't mean you have all the answers. It's actually the contrary—in our human, imperfect state we are void of understanding in many areas. What you being the solution means is that the One who has all the answers, the Ancient of Days, lives inside you!

God is raising up solutionists in our time who hold the keys to the biggest problems ailing society. How do you activate this dimension of power in your life? I believe it starts by identifying the things in your life or environment that bother you. Your assignment can be found in the thing that irritates you the most. For example, I can remember being upset by the lack of creative books and material on a particular subject. I'm a lover of books and learning. At that point over a decade ago, I noticed how in a specific genre some of the material was surface level, bland, and just outdated. This began to irritate me because I was looking for something I couldn't find. I'd recognize the knowledge and instruction I was looking for on the pages if I saw them, but I hadn't yet found them. The Lord kindly and gently allowed me to know, *That's because you (along with others) are called to write on that subject. You're the solution to this dilemma.*

At that moment, I stopped complaining and began to look at things with a spiritually sober mind. I realized the responsibility was on me to bring solutions to the area of my irritation. Just as I realized that God uses the things that bother me to point me toward my purpose, you too must awaken to that understanding. Your destiny and purpose are always revealed in trouble and problematic situations. Who you really are comes out under the right amount of pressure. Here are seven key principles to help activate solutions in your life:

1. Realize that you are anointed to help others.
2. Identify the problems in your life that continue to persist.
3. Identify the problems in your community that you are anointed and skilled to deal with.
4. Imagine how those situations in your life or community could be better.
5. Seek wisdom, do research, and gain information to help assist you in your mission.
6. Brainstorm ways that you can add positivity to those situations.
7. Effect change by being a vehicle God can use to bring light in the darkness.

You Are Multidimensional

Psalm 139:14 in the New Living Translation says, "Thank you for making me so wonderfully complex! Your workmanship is marvelous—how well I know it." I love how this is worded. The Holy Spirit inspired the author of this division of the psalms to describe a human being as wonderfully complex. *Complex* means consisting of many different and connected parts.[2] As you grow through life, one of the things you'll discover is that you are multidimensional, meaning you were created to operate in multiple capacities at the same time.

As a young teenager, when I became a serious believer in Christ, I didn't know you could be called to more than one spiritual assignment. Some religious institutions have done a disservice to believers by demonstrating that you should just find your role and stick to it. When I was coming up, there were only a few things to choose from in the Church. If you were musical, you were placed in the music department. If you were good with people, you could be a greeter, an usher, or possibly in a speaking role. If you were gifted at serving, exhorting, or preaching, you would typically be placed in a ministerial role. In some organizations, once these roles are defined, there is no further movement or progression. But you were never meant to serve in only one capacity.

Jesus was and is the greatest prophet, chief apostle, and cornerstone of the Church. During His earthly ministry, He was the most profound teacher, most compassionate evangelist, and most loving shepherd/pastor of those who were willing to come to Him. Yet He was a carpenter. Some say a better description would be a builder, possibly of houses. This would explain His language in comparing Himself to the cornerstone of a building, and other carpentry language He used. I'm sharing this example because it emphasizes the point that Jesus had many roles. He is our example in demonstrating the different dimensions we also may be called to.

You are not defined by the role you are in; you are much more than a title. You can be an actor and an evangelist. You can be a medical doctor and a prophet, if that combination is God's calling for you. You can be a minister and a lawyer. You can serve faithfully in your church and also be a successful entrepreneur. Don't limit how God desires to express Himself through you.

You Are Innovative

The word *innovate* means to introduce something new or make changes to something that is already established.[3] From the beginning of time, God made people to be creative and innovative. The world's greatest inventions, creations, and modifications have always come through the womb of a woman. We were made with a built-in creative ability.

Through the fallen nature of humanity, and through Satan, the god of this world, blinding people's eyes, pure creativity and innovation have been stifled in many people. When you accept Jesus into your heart, however, I believe that He not only saves you from destruction and redeems you; I believe He also restores your God-given innovation and supernatural creativity. You receive His divine wisdom on how to design on earth what He has already constructed in heaven. God's design of us as innovative and creative provides the access to bring heaven down to earth.

I believe innovation is the key to positioning and equipping the next generation. The world is far more advanced in the natural than sectors of the Church are. This is not how it should be, and not how God meant it to be. We believers will need innovative ideas to reach groups of people who have been brainwashed against the Church. Thankfully, the Holy Spirit is the master creator and innovator, and He lives on the inside of those of us who receive Him.

You Are God's Big Idea

An idea is a thought or concept about a possible course of action. It further means the aim or purpose of something.[4] Jeremiah 1:5 (ESV) says, "Before I formed you in the womb I knew you, and before you were born I consecrated you; I appointed you a prophet to the nations." God intimately and closely knows those whom He creates.

You were created by God, and you were with Him before He crafted and formed you in your mother's womb. You were an idea that came from God. Before He formed you, He thought of you, gave you a purpose, designed your course in life, and knew the skills and abilities you'd have. God put intentionality into meticulously constructing your destiny.

You are therefore God's big idea for managing and having dominion over the earth. You are God's big idea for stewarding His presence. You are God's big idea for carrying His glory and expressing His love to others. You are God's big idea to help someone else!

MANTLE MOMENT

As I mentioned earlier, God uses pressure to unlock who you really are. Sometimes our greatest solutions come forth in the most pressurized situations. One of the definitions for *mantle* is an important role or responsibility that passes from one person to another.[5] Jesus is the solution for the earth, and when He ascended into heaven, His Spirit was sent to now dwell in us. I believe that the mantle for solutions is within God's people, meaning that you and I carry a mantle for solutions. Your mantle just might need to be activated. Read back through the seven key principles to activate solutions that I listed for you earlier in this chapter. After following those steps, practice being the solution to a situation in some area of your life, whether on your job, amongst your family, or at your local church. Chronicle this experience, and answer these simple questions:

1. How did it make you feel to solve a challenging problem for someone?

2. How did the people affected by the problem feel after you were able to help bring them to a God-given solution?

3. What are some ways you can continue to show up as a solutionist in the world around you?

3

HELP! I'M CARRYING SOMETHING BIGGER THAN ME

"Not by might nor by power, but by my Spirit," says the LORD Almighty.

Zechariah 4:6 NIV

It was a grueling 17-hour, 22-minute flight. I was anxious, nervous, and excited all at the same time. My joints were slightly aching because of how long I had been scrunched in the little economy seat in the middle of the plane. The stewardess walked by and served what resembled a TV dinner. By this time, I was starving, so I was happy to see any food. I scarfed it down as quickly as I could, while I thought about what was about to transpire. When we landed and my feet touched the ground, I gave a sigh of relief. I muttered under my breath, *Thank You, God, for bringing my team and me safely to the continent of Africa.*

I journeyed to Zimbabwe and saw some of the most resilient people. At the time, they had an over 90 percent unemployment rate because their economy had collapsed. Their money became worthless. As I passed by the open market, I saw creativity, innovation, ingenuity—and sheer determination. The people were selling small trinkets, clothing, and anything they could find to make a living. I sat there with tears in my eyes. I thought of all the gifted and talented people I knew who were living in the United States, with access to comfort, convenience, and resources. I thought of myself. I had many goals and ideas that I had only lethargically pursued. I found myself completely broken and inspired at the same time by the strength of these beautiful people.

After this experience, I felt a mandate and burden for Africa, the continent of my ancestors. In the same year, I went to South Africa and toured, preaching at many churches from Johannesburg to Cape Town. I found that the churches there are filled with a hunger unparalleled by anything I've seen in the States. I've found this to be true with churches throughout Africa, from the southern tip to Nigeria, Kenya, Ghana, and beyond. The people know the Word of God, they are passionate in their worship and praise, and so many of them are desperate to see a move of God that they will pray all night. They will fast many days until they have an encounter with Jesus.

I preached in one town in Africa that was experiencing regular power outages. The people had grown accustomed to managing and working with what they had. I was on my way to a church when I got word that the power was out in the building. They had a few candles lit and were going strong in praise, worship, and prayer. When I walked into the building, it was almost pitch black, but I felt electricity hit my body. The presence and glory of the Lord was there. I was confounded at the people's hunger. I was adjusting myself to preach in the dark when the power of God hit the building. Right before I got up to minister, the electricity surged back on. I was told that it was the only building that had electricity in the whole town.

It was during this trip that I could feel the weightiness and burden of the mantle God had placed on my life for nations. I realized that I had this extremely big vision, a mandate and anointing that I couldn't run away from, and a calling that required me to give up everything to do the will of God for my life. On the other hand, back in the United States, I was pastoring a church that was only a few years old, trying to purchase a facility to house the volume of people we were now getting, and trying to juggle a demanding itinerant travel schedule. The Lord was doing amazing things, but I couldn't seem to birth out all these things God had placed in me. While there in Africa, I could feel the pressure of what I was carrying. I thought *Help, I'm carrying something that's bigger than me.* From then on, and for years afterward, the Holy Spirit would take me on a journey of realizing that what He placed in me is supposed to be too big for me. This meant that I must rely solely on Him in order to accomplish the vision.

It's Bigger Than You!

Likewise, it's important that you come to grips with the fact that the mantle, vision, mandate, and calling on your life is bigger than you. It's more than what your flesh can sustain, because it must be sustained by the Holy Spirit, and Him alone. Zechariah 4:6 (NIV) puts it this way: "'Not by might nor by power, but by my Spirit,' says the LORD Almighty."

Might and natural human effort, energy, or strength are not going to birth God's vision. It will be the Spirit of God flowing through you that will help you accomplish your purpose. One of the most profound things I've learned over the years is that the Holy Spirit desires to partner with you and me to bring to pass His agenda in the earth. Isn't that amazing?!

God wants to work with you to bring His will to pass for your life. So what do you do when you're overwhelmed, and you realize that what you're carrying feels too big? You *surrender*, you *prioritize*, you *examine your circle*, and you *delegate*. Let's look at each of these up close.

Surrender

When you come to the realization that what God placed on you is too big for you, it's a sign for you to fully surrender to Him. Give it back to the Lord; it's His assignment, vision, or calling, and He doesn't expect you to carry it alone.

The word *surrender* means "to yield (something) to the possession or power of another; deliver up possession of on demand."[1] It further means to give yourself up to some influence, course, force, or even emotion. When you fully surrender to God and His purpose, you are yielding to His unlimited power. Yielding allows His power to fully operate through you. His power is His ability, strength, wisdom, force, might, and Spirit infusing your life. Your vision, dream, God-idea, or mantle must always remain connected to the power source. That's the only way it receives life to function. Surrendering to God connects you to the power source.

When people refuse to surrender, they stop the flow of God's power. In 2 Timothy 3:5 (KJV), it's described as "having a form of godliness, but denying the power thereof." Anything less than full surrender to the Holy Spirit is simply having a form of godliness. For the anointing and mandate that God has placed on your life, you can't afford to be disconnected from His power. Surrender is the doorway to unlocking God's greatness in your life!

Prioritize

It's important that you prioritize your assignments and the things God has placed in your heart to do. I've noticed that many people get overwhelmed because they have not learned the importance of prioritizing. It's important that you understand that big vision is accomplished in phases. If you're going to take on something big, the only way to do it properly is in bite sizes.

Some years ago, I started a business renovating and flipping homes. It was exhilarating. Oftentimes, I would easily have a renovation budget of hundreds of thousands of dollars. The projects would feel enormous to me. I quickly learned from my construction crew, along with my general contractor, that the houses had to be completed in phases. First, we would do the redesign phase—putting the plans together for how we wanted a house to look and getting them approved by the city. Then, we would go in and gut the house in the demolition phase. This would require us to tear down walls and take out cabinets, flooring, and whatever else had to go to make the house eventually look more aesthetically pleasing. After that, we would work to seal up the house so no rain or outside elements could get inside. This phase consisted of repairing or replacing the roof, windows, and any entrances to the house. Next would be the framing of any walls, followed by electrical work, plumbing, and mud and tape. The last phase would be the fixtures, paints, and any other aesthetics to make the house look attractive.

In order to build or rebuild these houses, we would have to take each project in stages. In the same manner, you must take your vision and break it up into phases. This will help you not be so overwhelmed. In addition, you'll be able to track your progress as you pace yourself to accomplish your assignment. In Luke 14:28, Jesus says, "For which of you, desiring to build a tower, does not first sit down and count the cost, whether he has enough to finish it?" You must estimate what it will take you to complete the vision, strategically plan it out, and then go after it!

When you prioritize, start with the most important and time-sensitive task, and work from there. All assignments are not created equal. Some are greater than others and require more of your time and attention. When it comes to ministry, do the first thing God gave you to do first. Work from His order and not your own. God's order won't always make sense in the natural, but if you trust in the Lord, you'll never be disappointed with His results.

Examine Your Circle

The people you associate with can make or break your progression and forward movement. Make sure you're connected to people who have God's heart and your best interests at heart. Make sure you're surrounded by those who will build you up and not tear you down. You should be able to confide in your core circle of friends without them destroying your dreams and goals. You need people who will speak life into you and help unlock the greatness God has placed inside you, while you do the same for them.

One of the best pieces of advice on relationships is found in 1 Thessalonians 5:12 (KJV), which says to "know them which labour among you." This means that you must fully understand and clearly determine the traits of those who work with or are connected to you. You don't have to go year by year cutting people off; just know the people who are in your circle and place them in proper perspective, within proper boundaries.

Not everyone should be a core trusted person in your life. You may have only a very few people you can bare your soul to, and that's okay. In Scripture, David had Jonathan, Ruth had Naomi, Paul had Aquilla and Priscilla, and Daniel had Shadrach, Meshach, and Abednego. Your circle should be the support system you move through life with. These should be people God has sent, whom you are assigned to do life with.

The word *cycle* comes from the Greek word for *circle*.[2] A cycle is a series of events that is regularly repeated. By this understanding, whoever is in your circle helps create a cycle for your life. When you want to break a persistently destructive, negative cycle, sometimes it can only be broken by changing your circle. May God send you the right people who will join with you to accomplish your purpose.

Delegate

As a leader in business—managing several companies, being an employer with dozens of full-time, part-time, and contract employees, and also being a pastor—I've learned through my failure of trying to do it all alone. When God first gave me vision for what I'm now doing, I didn't have any help. I felt as though I had no one to help me facilitate the things God had called me to do. I went through a very frustrating season. Out of my frustration, I began to do what I had to do to get things done. I was my own admin person, graphic designer, publisher, event coordinator, and so forth. Although God only meant for this to be a short, temporary phase of learning to carry the vision no matter what, I developed this mindset of *I'll do it myself.*

When God gives you a mandate, however, you need a team of people who are committed to your vision in order for it to work. Your job is to convey the vision God gave you in a clear manner. Those who are called to it will come alongside you as you work on it.

Even if you start with three or four committed people who believe in your business, dream, or ministry vision, work with them. Then learn to delegate. This means that you identify the strengths of the people willing to work with you, and then you assign responsibilities and segments of the vision that they can oversee or work with. The only way you as a leader can do the great things that the Lord has placed within you is to learn to delegate.

Bringing Out the Lion within You

On my tour in Africa, I found myself on a safari. It didn't take much persuading to get me to go. For years, I had imagined what it would be like to see various animals in their native habitat in a place as beautiful as the area surrounding the town I was in. I climbed into a somewhat exposed safari vehicle. I looked at all of the possible openings, planning out security measures and being extra cautious. But I was excited to explore this desert terrain. What struck me on this exciting adventure were the massive lions that slowly moved about, with the majority of them arrayed out in the open. We had stumbled into a pride of lions. They were the most majestic creatures, seeming as though they owned the jungle.

I began to watch these lions in their natural habitat, and my guide instructed us on various facts about them. They had to be up to eight feet long, close to four feet tall, and must have weighed 300 to 400 pounds. Lions are the only cat species that lives in groups. A pride of lions can have up to thirty individuals. Most lions in the wild live on the continent of Africa. They are some of the most adaptable animals and can live in the driest climates. Because they are desert animals, they get most of their water from the prey they consume, and they will even get their water from plants. On average, lions feed every three to four days. They can go more than a week without food, but when they do eat, they can eat up to 50 kilograms of meat (or just over 110 pounds) at one time.

In Scripture, Jesus is referred to as the Lion of the Tribe of Judah (see Revelation 5:5). He was also the sacrificial Lamb that was slain for the sins of humanity, to reconcile the world back to God. He went to the cross as the Lamb, but when He arose on the third day, He got up as the Lion of Judah. Because Christ lives inside you, you are carrying the Lion of Judah within you. That is a representation of the greatness you carry. It's time for the Lion to arise in and through you.

The gifting and unique purpose you are carrying is activated by the Lion of Judah. By looking at the characteristics of lions, we can gain prophetic insight into how to navigate and unlock the greatness you hold on the inside.

- *Lions adapt to their environment.* Likewise, you must learn to adapt to any environment God places you in. Your mantle and anointing are limitless and thrive in the most difficult places.
- *Lions were made for the desert.* The Bible uses the terms *desert* and *wilderness* interchangeably. Lions instinctively navigate the desert, where some other animals couldn't survive. In this same way, you will manage every spiritual desert place you find yourself in and come out of it better.
- *Lions can eat one meal that carries them for days, without eating again.* When you consume the Word of God, it's timeless. It's a spiritual meal—one word from God's Word has the ability to carry you through multiple seasons. Even when you feel empty, you must realize that as long as you have the Word, you can never be without.
- *Lions live in groups.* Likewise, God has the right people for your life. You will experience help in your vision and assistance in your assignment as you join with other believers who are like-minded. There is strength in unity. Your God-given dreams can only be carried out with others who understand your assignment.
- *Lions are the kings of the animal kingdom.* Recognize that you too are royalty. You are a son or daughter of the King. This means you have authority and power from God. You have heaven backing you and your purpose. God has already ordered your steps, and your future is secure in Him.

In Christ, you have been equipped to carry and bring to fruition all that God has placed within your spirit. The Lion of Judah within you is awakening. Through Christ's Word, wisdom, and Spirit, you will birth your vision and see it come to pass!

MANTLE MOMENT

A mantle is designed to recognize, galvanize, and manifest your greatest potential. You were made to carry something that's bigger than you. You were made to shine a light to others. Earlier, I shared insight on what you do when you feel overwhelmed—as though you're carrying something that's too big. Those points were to surrender, prioritize, examine your circle, and delegate. Think of one situation that you believe God has put you in as an assignment that can sometimes feel overwhelming. Apply those four directives to what you're facing. Chronicle how these key points help you manage what God has placed in your hands.

4

A LITTLE BIT OF OIL

What shall I do for you? Tell me, what do you have in the house?

2 Kings 4:2

Whenever the Lord gets ready to reposition us or to put us in a new place, whether it's a spiritual promotion, a new assignment, or a new chapter or season, the anointing we possess—the anointing that is currently on us—must be upgraded for the new thing God is bringing us to. Over the years, I've watched many people whom God had anointed for one thing or one season try to progress to the next level with something stale and old. The Lord has said to me, *It's imperative that My people receive an upgrade.*

This word is for you: God is about to upgrade you—your anointing, the mantle under which you operate, or the assignment for which you've been sent. The Lord says, *It's time for you to receive that upgrade.* What worked for you seven years ago will not provide what you need today. What carried you into 2010 is not enough to carry you into the next year. Time is going by so quickly. According to what the Lord has spoken to my spirit, time has been accelerated. I don't know what day in the year it is for you as you read this book, but I want you to understand that you aren't simply preparing to enter a new day, month, or year. The Lord wants you to prepare your heart to think in terms of the next ten years.

Many times, as a new month, quarter, or year approaches, people set their sights on the next 30, 90, or 365 days. But you are not just anybody. You are a believer and a reformer, and the Lord is saying to you, *I've been preparing you for ten years beyond where you are today. I'm giving you a blueprint and a plan for you to be able to build what you see now so that it lasts into the future.*

You are not just building for now, for this season, or for what you see right in front of you. *You are building something now that will advance the Kingdom for years to come.* This means that you will need upgraded blueprints for you now, *and* for the generations that will be here to continue the work when you are long gone. Now is the time for you to begin to assemble people and pour into them, because you will need help to build, and to build with urgency this next thing God wants you to bring into the earth.

Now is also the time to have your level of anointing upgraded, which will help you handle the challenges, attacks, and warfare that come with the increased level of responsibility and influence God will give you. Looking ahead, there will be a new climate culturally, politically, spiritually, and economically that you will need divine strategy to navigate through. The anointing gives you access to the supernatural authority and wisdom needed to deal with these things. It breaks yokes and bondages and prepares the way for the things of God.

We have seen so many changes in the world and in our own nations. It's as if we are living in another place, or maybe as if we have time-jumped about twenty or thirty years in only the past two years. Why is that? It's because we are in an accelerated time. This is why God is calling for the builders, for those who can pick up the future, the assignment of heaven for what is to come, and begin to work in that direction.

Know What You Need

This is such a critical season in which the Lord wants to take the little bit you have and maximize it. We talked in chapter 1 about how every mega gift starts from a little concept, a little seed or idea. God has given you something that was enough for times past but is small compared to what He is about to do in the future. I want to share fresh revelation with you about this, and I'm going to deliver it through the biblical story of the woman who had just a little bit of oil. Her story, as recorded in 2 Kings 4:1–7, is a testimony of how God will use your currently small, ordinary thing and increase it many times over to bless you and others.

The Scriptures tell us a story about this woman—one of the wives of the men who attended the school of the prophets. Her husband had died, and she had run out of money. She was in debt, and the creditor was about to come take her two sons and put them to work as slaves until the debt was paid. She was so desperate to keep this from happening that she reached out to the prophet Elisha. The prophet came to her house, and when he learned of her situation, he said to her, "What shall I do for you? Tell me, what do you have in the house?" (2 Kings 4:2).

Now, if you've been a believer for some time, this is a story you've heard preached and have read for yourself many times. But what I want you to see is the prophetic revelation embedded within this text. Elisha asked this woman two important questions: "What shall I do for you?" and "What do you have in the house?" I believe God is about to bring you to places of divine opportunity where you will be asked, "What can I do for you?" You may never have experienced this before, but it's the same as when Solomon offered one thousand burnt offerings to the Lord and the Lord visited him in a dream, saying in effect, *Ask me for whatever you want* (see 1 Kings 3:5). These are once-in-a-lifetime opportunities where you are in a divine collision with destiny.

Many years ago, I had my very own collision with destiny. I was out ministering and began to prophesy in detail to this individual who I discovered later on was very wealthy. After the ministry session, this person came to me and said, "I want to meet with you. I want to do lunch with you." I agreed to the meeting, and when we sat down for lunch, this person said to me, "What do you need?"

I was stunned. Although I had begun preparation for the assignment the Lord was giving me, I never thought I would be asked a question like this. I wasn't prepared. Out of that situation, the Lord taught me to dream big, plan for greater, and always have an idea of what resources I need in order to accomplish the vision He has given me. I would later go on to receive a sizable monetary gift through this person, but it wasn't about the money. The greater lesson was recognizing the moment and being able to articulate what the needed provisions were.

You'll want to know what you currently have when God puts you in a situation where you're asked, "What do you need?" You'll want to know what's in your house, so you can articulate what you need. Divine opportunities are about to open up. You'll have encounters with destiny. There will be moments orchestrated by God's divine design that you didn't plan for or know were coming. You need to be ready for them when they come. You need to know what you need.

If you are in ministry, you need to know what you need to build out the vision God has given you. If you are an entrepreneur in business, you need to first understand God's assignment for you and why He has called you to build the business you're building. You'll also need to know what you need to make it successful, things like these: How much money does it take to operate this business? What will the overhead be? How many people will this business need to employ?

The Bible puts it this way: "For which of you, intending to build a tower, does not sit down first and count the cost, whether he has enough to finish it?" (Luke 14:28). So I'm asking you this question prophetically: *What do you need?*

As God brings you to this next season of mega, make a list of the things you need in order to accomplish the thing God has called you to. You need to make sure that every single detail is on that list, so that when you're asked what you need, you'll have the right answer.

What You Need, You Already Have

Getting back to the story that led us down this path, we read that the prophet Elisha asked the woman, "What do you have in the house?" She said, "Your maidservant has nothing in the house but a jar of oil" (2 Kings 4:2). She thought she didn't have much, but what she needed, she already had.

This is the moment in the story that I pray speaks to you. You may only have a little bit of something small in your possession. A little bit of oil may be symbolic of the small skill, the small talent, the little business, or the little ministry. For most people, their vision isn't the thing that's too small; it's the resources they have for it that may be too small. You may have looked at the vision the Lord has given you and said, "The vision is too big. I don't really have the finances. I don't have the resources. I don't have what it takes." But I want you to understand this: God is going to breathe on the small things. He is about to use the little you have and multiply it. He will use what's been embedded within your house, your spiritual house. It's already there.

Let me say this prophetically: There is a coming movement of those who have just a little bit of oil. God is saying, *I have already moved on those who have a lot. They're already governing many areas of industry, religion, and culture. The time has come for Me now to begin to breathe on those who say, "God, I only have a little—a little oil, a little anointing, a little skill."*

I can think back to years ago when I felt as if I had absolutely nothing. I felt as if all I could do was prophesy, and that was my response back in the day. People would ask me, "What's your skill? What can you do?" And I used to say to them, "Well, all I do is prophesy." Invitations would be extended to me for different things, and I didn't understand the power and potency of what the Lord had placed in me. I couldn't see the value in the little bit, because it looked small to me.

The Lord has placed significant value in you too, but maybe you can't see your value because what you have looks so small. You can't see your value because other people have looked over what you have and haven't recognize it. Yet the Lord specializes in hiding the most valuable possessions in secret places until the right time. Even as I used to say "all I do is prophesy," the Lord was saying, *That's all I need from you. All I need is the little bit that you have.*

The widow woman said, "I have nothing in the house but a jar of oil." Like her, you may be saying, *God, I have nothing but this little bit of oil.* And God is saying, *I'm going to breathe on that.*

We are about to witness the movement of the little bit. God is about to move on the thing you said was too small and insignificant. God places His power in the small thing. You may have always been in the company of people who have mega gifts and mega talents, and you've come to God and said, *But, God, I can't do what they can do. I'm not anointed like that. I don't see like that. I don't prophesy like that. My business is small. I don't have a huge company.*

Rather than validating what you see as small, the Lord says, *I have given you exactly what you need.*

Follow the Prophetic Instructions

Now, let's read the rest of the widow's story, because it's going to come alive in your spirit. "Go, borrow vessels from everywhere," the prophet told her (2 Kings 4:3). The key here is that you must listen to the instruction of the Lord and do what He says. When you only have the little thing—the little bit of oil, the little skill, the little talent, the little ministry, or the little business, it's imperative that you follow the prophetic instructions of the Lord for your life.

Elisha instructs the woman to go borrow vessels from everywhere. In essence, God was saying, *I'm about to perform miracles and release abundance in your life from borrowed vessels.* In other words, it's going to be a partnership with vessels that you've borrowed—vessels you don't even own. Your next download and the next wave you'll receive is going to be from borrowed vessels. It's going to be from those who will say, "Well, I can lend you this. Let me just lend you this opportunity. Let me just give you this, but you have to give it back to me."

Here's another key: The vessels you collect and borrow can't be full; they must be empty. You may be saying, *God, I'm empty right now. I don't have anything. I'm depleted and burned out. There's nothing in me. I'm so empty.* The Bible often refers to people God uses as vessels. This just means you are like a container created for the Master's use. So if you find yourself feeling empty, the Lord is saying, *This is exactly where I want you. I need empty vessels right now so I can fill you. If you're already full, I can't pour this next download into your spirit.*

In the next part of Elisha's instructions, he told the widow, "Do not gather just a few" (verse 3). This is the guiding principle of the entire prophetic instruction, which says that however many vessels the woman was able to gather would determine how much oil she would be able to hold. Your next download isn't based on how much God wants to give you. Your next download is based on how many vessels you can gather or hold.

What Is Your Capacity?

If you discover that you don't have the capacity to hold what God is bringing to you, then you need to go get more vessels. Vessels are structures for housing something. A vessel can be a person, an organization, or anything used to receive and pour into something else. The houses the woman went to when she was borrowing the vessels represent the world, spheres, systems, and circles that operate within the earth.

Put yourself in this woman's shoes. Can you imagine running to every house in your neighborhood, trying to collect as many vessels as you can carry, just to go back and ask for more? Think about it like this: If you only get a few vessels, your breakthrough will be limited to the few you have gathered. So there would be an urgency to get as many as you could.

In 2 Kings 4:4, Elisha tells the woman, "And when you have come in, you shall shut the door behind you and your sons; then pour it into all those vessels, and set aside the full ones." There are several more keys in here. Let's unpack them. First, the woman had to go get as many vessels as she could. In this, the Lord addressed her capacity. He was saying, *If you want to house more, I'll give it to you, but what I give will be according to what you're able to hold.* And just as it was for this woman, God is also addressing our capacity. How much can we hold? We say we want abundance, but do we have room for it in our house? We want revelation, but do we have room in our schedules for God to pull us in for hours and days of prayer, so we can receive from Him?

Do we have the capacity for the next dimension? Do we have the capacity for the next level? This must be addressed first. You need to answer the question of capacity in your life. If there is no room for more, you need to start clearing stuff out. You need to start clearing your schedule for time with God. You need to make room in your life. Why? Because the Lord is trying to prepare you for the next download.

Go into Your Own House and Shut the Door

Let's go to the next part of the story. Once the woman and her sons got the vessels, they did as they were instructed. They came back to their own house, not somebody else's house. They didn't go into somebody else's house to help them with their project. This is a word for you: Don't enter into somebody else's assignment. Go back into your house, where you have your jar of oil. Your house is a space made up of what you possess. Your body is known as the house of God.

There were times in my life when the Lord had given me an assignment and I felt that the assignment, or what I was doing, was insignificant. It felt empty, so I wanted to run into somebody else's house. But this story shows us that we have to go into our own house. Then the next part of this step is to "shut the door behind you" (verse 4). We're in one of these seasons where we will need to shut doors behind us. We must move forward and not return to the things of the past. There are some places and spaces that only you and your sons—representing those who are assigned to you and connected to you—can enter.

The key here is that God is not going to shut the door. You'll have to shut the door behind you in the faces of people who are not assigned to you. They are not ordained to access what the Lord has placed in your hands. This may be hard to receive, and it's not personal. It's just purpose. You're not upset with these people. They may not have done anything to you; your assignment just doesn't include them at this time. There's something the Lord is trying to do in you and in your house, and what He's doing for you is not for everyone you know or meet.

There are doors you will need to shut to certain connections and relationships, but then there are other doors you must shut in your life to anything that is an enemy of God. Doors will need to be shut to doubt and fear. Doors will need to be shut to the voices that speak contrary to the word of the Lord in your life. Doors must be closed to complaining and murmuring, and doors must be closed to sickness and disease.

Then there are doors to spiritual attack that must be shut. Certain attacks may have followed you for years or even decades of your life, but you are going to shut the door right now.

Finally, you will need to shut the door to anything that has embedded itself in your bloodline to hinder you from living in the fullness of God's promises. There are curses that have been in your bloodline—like curses of premature death or extreme poverty. You may have had a curse in your bloodline that causes you to lose everything the moment you start accumulating it. That curse is about to stop now because you're going to shut the door on the enemy. You're about to shut the door to generational poverty, and now you're going to begin to create generational wealth.

None of these things can enter this mega season with you. They end right here. Shutting the door to the past may look like walking away from negative or toxic situations, or even people whom the enemy has tried to use. Sometimes you must learn to love toxic people within boundaries—from afar. Shutting the door may look like ending a cycle, period, or pattern of behavior that is not adding value to you or your assignment. When you close doors, metaphorically you are saying, *I'm putting an end to this particular thing.*

God is saying, *Shut the door. Whatever you need to close the door to in your life, close it now.* Hear the word of the Lord.

Listen and obey. Shut the door behind you, because we are now about to enter such a significant time that will be filled with the manifested promises of God, and there are some things we cannot afford to bring with us.

It's Time to Pour

As the Scripture passage continues, we learn that the woman had yet another step to carry out. Once she had gone into her house and shut the door, then she had to "pour it into all those vessels" (verse 4). There was a lot of work involved in getting all those vessels from the neighbors' houses back to her own house. She and her sons must have been tired. But this wasn't the time for them to get inside and start relaxing: "Oh, thank God! We made it back to the house. Let's just relax and kick back."

No! The instruction came immediately, saying, *When you've shut the door behind you, start pouring.* Realize that if you waste time getting started on the pouring, you're going to miss out on some of the overflow you should be receiving. We're coming into a period of time where the Lord will say, *It's time to pour.* And He's asking you to pour what was little—the little bit of oil that was in the jar—into the vessels.

If you're called to ministry, if you're a prophet, apostle, pastor, or another ministry leader, the Lord says, *You are in a season of pouring.* If you aren't already mentoring someone, you're about to step into it now. You're about to start raising up and training people. Through groups, seminars, intensives, and schools, you're about to pour into people because it's the time.

Don't Limit the Pour

If you limit the pour by failing to assemble the containers or vessels, you will limit the overflow. The Bible says that the widow left Elisha and shut the door behind her, along with her sons, who had brought the borrowed vessels to her. She started pouring the little bit of oil she had into all those vessels, and she set aside the full ones. Look what happened next: "Now it came to pass, when the vessels were full, that she said to her son, 'Bring me another vessel.' And he said to her, 'There is not another vessel.' So the oil ceased" (2 Kings 4:6). The oil stopped when the vessels stopped.

I say this to you as an apostolic admonition and instruction: Gather as many vessels as you can. Why? Because the oil stops when there's nothing else to pour it into. As I mentioned earlier, vessels can represent people or structures such as buildings or houses. There are also times that vessels represent intangible concepts like infrastructures. So a vessel in your case is anything that can house something. God may send you out into the marketplace or into any other type of system and say to you, *Gather. Don't stop at just one. Don't stop at just two. I know you've already built something, and it took all your energy. You planted that church, but there's another one for you to plant after that.*

God is challenging us to gather more, because if we can gather the vessels, then the oil will just keep flowing. What we see here in this Scripture story is that the oil didn't run dry as long as the widow kept pouring into vessels. There's a parallel of this same type of miracle in 1 Kings 17:8–16, where another widow with only a little bit of oil served a meal to the prophet Elijah, and then the oil she had also didn't run dry. I'm telling you prophetically today that the Lord will give you a supply of new oil. He will take the little bit you had and upgrade what you've been carrying so your oil will not run dry.

Discerning Your Oily Season

How do you know when the Lord is about to bring you into a season that's just oily? How do you know when God is about to download fresh oil into your life? These are good questions because there is a process for the oil.

Have you ever been to Israel, to the Garden of Gethsemane, to be precise? I have. There was a time I would go every year. I've stood in the Garden of Gethsemane. Of course, we know that's where Jesus engaged in one of the most profound battles in prayer, where there was blood dripping like sweat down His face as He interceded. One of the most amazing things about this garden is the olive trees. They are more than two thousand years old. They've been there from the very time when Jesus was there. One of the times I was standing there, I watched as several workers came out and began to shake the trees. I found this so interesting. The trees were full of olives. Ripe and ready, they began to fall off the trees. The workers quickly gathered them all, and I imagine they were taken to an olive press to produce the most anointed oil from those two-thousand-year-old trees that our Savior once knelt under, pouring His heart out to His Father.

This battle in prayer was Jesus' pressing process, much like what those olives may have gone through after they'd been harvested. It's important to understand that when you want to harvest olives, you cannot just pick them from the tree. The olive has a built-in mechanism where if it's picked from the tree, that act releases poison into the olive. In other words, the chemical makeup is altered whenever an olive is plucked from a tree. To preserve the integrity of the fruit and the oil, olives can only be harvested by shaking the tree. So I say this to you: The way you know that you're about to receive a download of fresh oil from God is that your tree will be shaken. As the saying goes, everything that can be shaken will be shaken. You'll be in a season where it will feel as if you're being dropped. You were in the high place. Then all of a sudden, because of the shaking that came, you were dropped. This is the beginning of the process of making the oil.

You know this sort of season. You've been here before. There have been periods when you've said, *God, it seems as though I keep going through one shaking after another.* You've watched other people who seem as though they've been selected to display their talents or gifts. Somebody came and picked them and said, "Oh, this is the one!" But the Lord says to you, *Your anointing is not coming by somebody picking you. Your anointing cannot be picked by human hands. The anointing that's about to come on you is coming from the shaking you've endured in this last season.*

You thought it was just a shaking, but God says that an upgrade has been embedded in the shaking. The shaking is the process for the overflow of the oil that is about to flow from your life, and God is not going to waste a shaking period.

Get Ready for a Divine Upgrade

If you've been in a shaking, get ready for the oil to come flowing out. You may have been going through a shaking in your personal life, in your ministry, in your family. We've been going through a shaking in my country, the United States. These shakings are a prophetic sign that the oil of anointing is about to flow.

The Lord has said to me that *we're about to see the emergence of new oil from all we just went through.* Now, understand this: The Lord said about what we endured at the beginning of the 2020 decade, *I'm not going to waste that.* There's been so much loss, and the Lord said, *You better start counting up the things you lost. You need to start counting up what it looks as if you lost, because you actually didn't lose it. It's going to meet you in another season of your life. It's about to find you in the next season of your ministry or in the next chapter of your marriage. What you thought you lost, you really did not lose. It was just the shaking producing an anointing out of you. You're about to experience an upgrade.*

I prophesy an upgrade to you right now. This is your time. You may see it manifest naturally. Whenever the Lord starts releasing spiritual upgrades, many times it manifests in the natural. For example, where you weren't even looking for new vehicles, but they just came. You weren't even looking for a new house, but the Lord just sent a new property. You weren't even looking for a promotion on the job, but it just came. Many times, these are signs of a spiritual upgrade happening at the same time.

I prophesy that a divine upgrade will come over you within hours, days, weeks, and months of reading these words. If you know my ministry, you know that historically, I do not release words like this. I'm not the kind of prophet and apostle who releases these kinds of words. As a matter of fact, I'm careful not to give these kinds of words, but the Lord said to release this word now. This is no gimmick. This upgrade is just going to find you. It will seem as if it's coming out of nowhere. Get ready to testify. Share it everywhere and with everyone. Let others know what God is doing in your life. Tell them, "This is my upgrade season."

The Lord says, *I'm taking the little bit, and I'm about to stretch that thing out. I'm taking the little skill you have, and I'm about to stretch it out. You will experience upgrade.*

Your oil is not going to run dry in this season. You may feel as though you've been depleted. You may have been working so hard. I know you've been plowing, you've been pushing, and you've been working. You've been taking care of your family and those around you. You've been covering those in your ministry, and I know you feel depleted. You may even feel as though you've given your last, or you don't really have much left. The Lord says, *The little you do have, I'm going to breathe on that, and I'm going to cause it to stretch and work for you.*

Receive the refreshing from God in your life. Declare aloud right now, "My oil will not run dry. Lord, You are giving me fresh oil and new strategies. New anointing is coming upon me right now, in the name of Jesus."

MANTLE MOMENT

Everyone has something valuable God has placed within them, even if it seems small or insignificant. God specializes in taking those kinds of things and making them shine. The story of the multiplication of oil that I referenced in this chapter is so relevant today. Here are some questions you can answer that will help you discover your oil and see God's hand of multiplication in it:

1. What do you have in your house (that can benefit you and others)?
2. What do you need?
3. What do you need to accomplish?
4. What are God's instructions for this season of your life?
5. What is your capacity?

5

PIVOT

And He said to them, "Cast the net on the right side of the boat, and you will find some." So they cast, and now they were not able to draw it in because of the multitude of fish.

John 21:6

In Luke 5:1–7, we're brought in on a scene where Jesus had been teaching multitudes of people all day long. The crowds had begun to press in closer and closer to hear the word of the Lord. They had pressed in so much that Jesus, initially standing on the lakeshore, had climbed into a fishing boat and asked the fisherman, Simon, to "put out a little from the land" to give some distance between the people and Himself (verse 3). Perhaps feeling a little more comfortable, Jesus sat down in the boat and continued teaching.

When He finally ended His message, Jesus told Simon, "Launch out into the deep and let down your nets for a catch" (verse 4). Simon let Jesus know that they had already been fishing in those waters—all night, to be exact—and had not caught anything. Then Simon said, ". . . nevertheless at Your word I will let down the net" (verse 5). Note Simon's obedience.

The Bible then reports, "And when they had done this, they caught a great number of fish, and their net was breaking. So they signaled to their partners in the other boat to come and help them. And they came and filled both the boats, so that they began to sink" (verses 6–7).

What an introduction Jesus made of Himself to these men, who would soon afterward become His disciples. This net-breaking miracle didn't happen just once, either. Shortly after dying on the cross and being resurrected, Jesus had gone around revealing His resurrected self to different groups of His followers. In John 21:1–8 we read about a particular time when He returned to a certain group of His followers to show Himself again. Simon Peter was included in this number. We read that Peter had decided to go fishing, and the rest of the group had wanted to go, too. We also read that as before, the men had been out on the boat all night and had caught nothing. Verses 4–6 tell us,

> When the morning had now come, Jesus stood on the shore; yet the disciples did not know that it was Jesus. Then Jesus said to them, "Children, have you any food?"
>
> They answered Him, "No."
>
> And He said to them, "Cast the net on the right side of the boat, and you will find some." So they cast, and now they were not able to draw it in because of the multitude of fish.

What I want you to know about this is that this same thing is about to occur in your life. You've been warring in one area and you're worn out, but God says, *Make the shift. It's time to pivot.*

The word *pivot* means "a usually marked change," or "an adjustment or modification made (as to a product, service, or strategy) in order to adapt or improve."[1] Understand this: The disciples were fishing all night long and they couldn't catch anything. Jesus came to them and began to speak the word right in the place where they had had the greatest disappointment. Then He told them to cast their net on the other side. That's a pivot. In essence, He was saying, *You had your net on this side, but I want you to cast your net on the other side.* When they did as He commanded, the thing they had been toiling for all night long manifested in abundance. Because they made a slight adjustment, a slight change, the Lord opened the floodgates for them.

I sense God saying that for you, this season is all about the strategic pivot. You're going to make decisions that will bring about revolutionary change in your life. You've been working in one area, in one field, on one side of the boat, and the Lord is going to cause you to step over into another field, to cast your net on the other side. When you obey God and make that pivot, you're going to experience a great harvest.

To walk in the overflow that comes from the pivot, some changes must be made. You may have to make an adjustment in your relationships. You may need to make an adjustment when it comes to your ministry. Maybe you've been focusing on one area, but the Lord is saying, *Now, I want you to turn your attention into this area. This is going to be the new assignment. Make the shift.*

The shift is already upon us, but you must be willing to take a risk in order to reap the harvest that accompanies it.

Another Way

If you're anything like me, you may serve the Body of Christ—your local church—as an evangelist, prophet, pastor, or teacher, but there's more to you than just that. Although I minister prophetically and apostolically, I also have several businesses. During one particular season, I was focused on one specific business more than the others. As I approached the new year, the Lord began to give me dreams and visions concerning another venture I had started but hadn't put much energy into. One night, the Lord interrupted my sleep to show me a vision of this venture. He said, *This is the area that you are about to push in. You thought I was going to come in this way with the harvest, but there is another way.*

You may have been weighing different directions for the next move in your business or ministry. You've looked at one thing, but another thing seems to be on the horizon. If this is the kind of prayer you've taken up with God, where you've been focused on one particular way ahead, I think you need to hear the same word God spoke to me: *There is another way.* You've been pushing in one area, and you've put everything into that one thing. If this is you, you're about to see God open up another avenue. You're about to make a shift.

Perhaps you've been praying about a venture or an opportunity, asking, *Lord, should I do this now? Should I start it now? When should I go into it?*

The Lord is saying, *Do it now.* Because when you do it in this season, the wind of God will blow on it.

This word is not for everyone. But if this word is connecting with your spirit, when you make the pivot God is calling you to make, He will breathe on it and you will see the manifestation and the result of what He has promised. Just know this: Harvest is coming another way.

We must begin to expand our minds. We must step back and ask the Lord, *Which way are you going to bring the promise to pass? Which way are you going to manifest the vision you've given me?*

We must stay connected to God to know what direction to pivot in, what change to make, and how to shift. We may be expecting breakthrough, deliverance, victory, or provision to come through one door, but there is another door. We may expect it to come from one avenue, but there is another.

Your strategy in the past may have been to fight, but in this season, God is telling you, as He told the people of Israel, *I have another way. Instead of fighting, position yourself, stand still, and see My salvation* (see Exodus 14:13; 2 Chronicles 20:17). He is saying, *Stand and see My deliverance. See Me break you through. See Me manifest My promises to you. Yes, I am bringing My promises to pass for you, but they're coming in a way you weren't expecting.*

When the Lord began to give me visions and dreams about this other business venture I hadn't thought much about, I began to do as God said and make the pivot in my business model. He let me know that what I had begun to put together wasn't limited to one industry. *I'm putting you into multiple industries*, He said. *In other words, I'm opening up multiple streams for you.* That pivot opened up a stream of income far beyond what I had seen in the past. Only God could do something as amazing as that! And He gets all the glory for it.

Moving in the right timing with God and sensing His call to you to make even a slight change is so critical for you in this season. You must stay connected to the heart of God. You must seek Him for what He is telling you to shift into now. What is the thing that He wants you to do, and what is the strategy to accomplish it?

Seven Keys to Pivoting with God

Everything you do in this season must be carried out strategically, so I want to shift now and share seven keys with you on how to pivot with God successfully. These keys are to (1) *move with the momentum*, (2) *discern the time*, (3) *proceed in stealth mode*, (4) *put on the garment of humility*, (5) *consecrate yourself*, (6) *celebrate anyway*, and (7) *stay focused*. We'll look at each key individually because I want you to know how to align with God in this season to pull in a harvest so big that, like the disciples, you'll need to call others to come by and help you gather it.

1. Move with the momentum.

The glory of God in a place or on a thing or person is an indication of His presence. God is everywhere His glory is. God's glory is His manifested presence. Where God and His glory are, strength, provision, protection, wisdom, and so much more are also there. In Scripture, God's glory is also His goodness. So when you see the glory of God on something—when God highlights a thing to you in this season—you must move on that thing. When you see the heavens open over one thing more than another, you get on that thing and not the other. You must move with the momentum of heaven.

You may be praying, *God, I have all these ideas. Which one should I do?* Or you may pray, *You've put all these gifts and talents in me, but I don't even know where to start.*

God is saying, *Move with the momentum. Move with the one you sense My glory on.* Because when the glory of the Lord is over a thing, you don't have to put in as much effort. There's an ease that comes in the glory. When the glory of God is over a thing, you're not going to have to work as hard.

2. Discern the time.

"For everything there is a season, a time for every activity under heaven" (Ecclesiastes 3:1 NLT). As you move with God, acting on His instruction to pivot, you must know what you can say, what you shouldn't say, when to say what you should say, and when to stay silent.

There are some things the Lord will tell you to keep under wraps, and you must do it. There are some things you won't be able to open your mouth about, some things you can't tell people about. You're going to have to hold it. There are things the Lord is incubating in you that you're not released or authorized to say. If you say it prematurely, it's going to be out of timing. If you act on it prematurely, you're going to miss the momentum you would have had in the right time. Knowing the timing of the Lord in this way is critical. This kind of knowing comes with discernment.

Ecclesiastes 9:12 tells us that a person who doesn't know his or her time is like a fish caught in a net. When you don't understand the season and the timing of God, you become trapped by what you don't know. This is the reason why it's information that unlocks you into a new season. Because when you discern the timing of God, it opens you up into another place—the new possibilities that manifest themselves in the shift.

When you don't know your timing, you're trapped. You may be feeling stuck or as if you're trapped because you couldn't discern the timing of the Lord. God is now giving you illumination and revelation. He is opening up your eyes to discern that the time is now. You have stepped into a season of pivoting.

3. Proceed in stealth mode.

Much as I just said, you must discern what you should and shouldn't say, because this will also be a season when what you do in private will draw God's open, public reward. For the secret prayers you've prayed privately, He is going to reward you openly. It's imperative during this season that you don't broadcast what you're giving and what you're sowing. Give in private, and now hear the Lord saying, *I'm going to reward you openly.* When we broadcast and say those things out of the timing of God, then the reaction we get from people is our reward.

This is a season when you must move in stealth mode. God may ask you to plant seeds into people's lives, and you're not going to broadcast it. You won't say, "I just gave them this." You might buy food for families, but you're going to keep it under wraps. You might give gifts to families in need, but you must keep it silent, because the blessing is coming out of the silence. This way, God gets the glory.

4. Put on the garment of humility.

When God blesses you in a big way and begins to fulfill long-awaited promises, it's imperative that we humble ourselves. Anytime we come to the close of a season and get ready to enter a new one, we have to find humility again. We must begin to put on the garment of humility. This is not the time or the season for us to be lifted up in pride. The Bible tells us in several key places that the one who exalts himself (or herself) will be humbled, or made low, and the one who humbles himself will be raised up or exalted (see Matthew 23:12).

There have been times when the Lord has had me in this space where He has said, *You're going to humble yourself in these areas, or I'm going to humble you.* There's a difference between you humbling yourself and God humbling you. There's a difference between you putting on the garment of humility and when the Lord has to break pride out of you. You don't want to get to a place where the Lord has to humble you.

Approaching this new chapter or phase, we're stepping over into a place of strategic moves, and we must come in humility. There are people whom the Lord is going to push you to apologize to, and it's not so much about them as it is about your humility. It's about a garment of humility. There are people about whom the Lord will tell you, *I want you to go and be a blessing to them.*

You may say, *But, God, why would I be a blessing to them when they've done me harm?*

Then the Lord is going to say, *I'm testing your humility.*

Can I be personal for a second here, for the purpose of teaching? There are people who have completely betrayed me and stabbed me in the back, but the Lord has said to me, *I want you to help them.* In these situations I don't question God, because whenever the Lord pushes me into things like this, not only is it about getting a blessing to that individual and the Lord showing that person grace and mercy; it is also about the Lord testing my obedience.

God tests us to see if we're going to obey Him anyway. He wants to train us to rise above the pain in our flesh. He wants us to rise above what somebody said or did to us, and still do what He is telling us to do.

You may be on the receiving end of a test like this. You must pass the test, because when you pass, you are then going to reap the benefits. Humility is the key. As we are in this season of pivoting, we must move through it with the right heart and the right motive.

5. Consecrate yourself.

David, the psalmist, was always so authentic with God. With all the things David did that many find contrary to God and His ways, God still called him a man after His own heart (see 1 Samuel 13:14; Acts 13:22). Though God dealt with David as a son, chastising and correcting him when he needed it, God also continued to prosper him throughout his life. Maybe it was humble prayers that kept David in God's favor, prayers like "Create in me a clean heart, O God, and renew a steadfast spirit within me" (Psalm 51:10), or "Search me, O God, and know my heart! Try me and know my thoughts!" (Psalm 139:23 ESV).

I believe we need to remain in the posture of humility and consecration, whether we're in a season of change or not. As chosen ones whose one desire is to please the Lord, we should be coming to Him and praying, *Lord, if there's something in me that's not like You, Father, take it out. I want to be like You. I want to be one with You so that the enemy doesn't find anything in me when he comes searching.* Let this always be our posture, because when it's time to pivot, then we won't miss God. We will be so tuned-in to Him that we will hear His still, small voice saying to us, *It's time to move. I'm over here. Come up higher.*

I love Joshua 3:5 (ESV), which says, "Consecrate yourselves, for tomorrow the Lord will do wonders among you." Consecration is the spiritual process that purifies the heart. It is the doorway to accessing the supernatural wonders of God. The word *consecrate* comes from a Hebrew word that means to clean, prepare, and purify.[2]

God is about to do unusual, unheard-of, seemingly impossible, miraculous wonders in your life. All you have to do is posture yourself for the pivot. Let God prepare your heart. What He has coming your way is going to happen so fast. You've been plowing and fishing and haven't caught anything, but you won't stay in that dead-end place forever. God is about to break you out and do wonders for you.

6. Celebrate anyway.

We've discussed putting on the garment of humility and consecrating ourselves, and you've done this. You've humbled yourself. You've been in seasons where you've been made low. You may be in a season now where it seems as though everybody else around you, even the one who did you wrong, is being elevated. You're praying. You've gotten your heart right. And it's like, *Lord, I don't understand where You have me, but I'm going to celebrate anyway. I'm going to celebrate with those who are celebrating. I'm going to push forward with those who are moving forward. I'm making the decision to keep my heart pure.*

Do just as His Word says: "Rejoice with those who rejoice" (Romans 12:15), because God sees. Your pure motive is an act of faith that God responds to. Your behavior testifies of your trust in God's plan for your life, that you know your times are in His hands, and that He has an expected end for you (see Jeremiah 29:11).

It takes humility to trust God and put your life completely in His hands. God sees this. He sees you, and He is saying, *Now I'm going to raise you up. I'm going to exalt you.* For as James 4:10 (ESV) says, "Humble yourselves before the Lord, and he will exalt you."

7. Stay focused.

The final key before we leave this chapter is to stay focused. Even though the pivot is marked by a major overflow of blessings, the Lord also told me that in this season, there will be another shaking in the world and within our countries and communities. In this period, there will be unearthing and a disruption within the earth. While some are going to be focused on that disruption, and some are going to be focused on what's going on out there, you need to keep your focus. You must focus on the agenda and assignment of God.

Pull your mind in and refuse to be distracted by the things around you. Push forward with what the Lord is doing and the thing He has given you. You are coming into the greatest pivot season of your life. You are going to make a shift that will open up the floodgates of heaven over you.

Listen, this word is for you. I want you to take it and build with it. Take the risk and make the change and adjustment God is directing you to make. When you do this, you will see God give you one of the greatest catches you've ever received.

MANTLE MOMENT

Every great leader in Scripture had to shift with the new thing that God did in his or her life. Joshua had to pivot when Moses was taken off the scene and it was his turn to lead. Elisha had to pivot when he received the mantle from Elijah. He shifted from being a follower at the school of the prophets to stepping into the shoes of his mentor. Mary had to pivot when she became pregnant with Jesus before she could marry her betrothed, Joseph. And Joseph had to pivot, too! What strategic pivot do you sense God is asking you to make? What is your plan to navigate the changes and discomfort that come with this pivotal change? How do you plan to move forward?

6

THE CEILING IS BREAKING

And thy heaven that is over thy head shall be brass, and the earth that is under thee shall be iron.

Deuteronomy 28:23 KJV

When the Lord calls you into the deep, into a vision, purpose, or assignment that is bigger than you, He will give you revelation and strategy that help you build the capacity to house and steward what He has given you. Some time ago, I was feeling the weight of all God was calling me to. I had experienced a level of acceleration and had seen lots of opportunity come into my ministry. But then it was almost as though I hit a ceiling or plateau. While pivoting was something God had instructed me to do in times past, this season was different. There was something more He wanted to reveal to me. This time, it wasn't about changing directions; this time, it was about staying the course and breaking through.

If you stick with God long enough, there will be times along your journey to fulfilling your God-sized vision, purpose, or assignment when you begin to feel as though you've reached a dead end and you're unsure how to continue. On the one hand, God may be calling you to pivot—to change directions and cast your net on the other side of the boat, as we saw in the previous chapter. But on the other hand, there are other times when God wants to reveal something more.

Seasons when it feels as if doors are closed or breakthrough is held up can cycle in and out of a believer's life as you go from glory to glory. There's a perfect saying that sums up part of what this dynamic can be: *new levels, new devils*. Have you heard this? Opposition may increase at times, but so does the refining and pruning that God may be doing in your life to grow your character so you're able to handle the capacity and weight of what He is bringing to you.

If you're feeling as though you have pivoted and God has blessed you, but you have now hit a ceiling or a plateau, let me reassure you that you're not crazy. Yes, you have seen and experienced great things in God, but you're also right that there's more.

When I was experiencing this, I sought the Lord in prayer about what this dead-end feeling is. I delivered the word He gave me about it to my church one Sunday, and the whole place erupted. In this chapter, I want to share this same revelation with you. I believe God told me about seasons like this to give us more clarity and insight about what to do when it seems as though all the doors in our lives are closed.

Before I take you through all He shared with me, however, I want to give you the punch line, the spoiler, about where you will be if you hold on. God said, *Tell the people that the ceiling is breaking over them. That plateau they've gotten to, that place where it seems as if they're praying, but their prayers are just going to the ceiling and back down, that place where it seems as if they've gotten to a certain level, but they just cannot get past it . . . Tell them they're about to see that limitation, that ceiling over them shatter.*

You might want to pause right here and thank God for this word. He is shattering any restriction or limitation that has blocked you.

A Closed Heaven

The feeling that you're hitting a plateau or ceiling is identified in the Bible as a closed heaven. Comparing a closed heaven to brass—a very hard-to-penetrate alloy metal, Deuteronomy 28:23 (KJV) says, "And thy heaven that is over thy head shall be brass, and the earth that is under thee shall be iron." This verse highlights a very important relationship—one between heaven and earth. It tells us that the heavens affect the earth, and that when the heavens are brass, meaning they are closed, nothing gets through. When heaven is closed, earth dries up.

If you are under a closed heaven, you've entered a place of a spiritual drought. When Scripture describes this point in a believer's life, it isn't speaking literally; it's talking about a time when the spiritual atmosphere over your life has been shut up, where the heavens over you have been shut up to the point that there's nothing coming down into your life and nothing going up. It's talking about times when you pray and it seems as if nothing is getting through, and the answers you seek from God are not coming back down to you.

I want to explore two main reasons why you may be under what the Bible calls a closed heaven, or a heaven that has been shut up. One has to do with the Church, in the form of religious oppression. The other has to do with you, in the form of unconfessed and unconfronted sin in yourself or in your family line. Let's look at each of these reasons more closely.

Religious Oppression

On October 31, 1517, the German priest, theologian, monk, and author Martin Luther nailed his *Ninety-five Theses* on the door of Castle Church, also known as All Saints' Church, in Wittenberg, Germany. Considered a rebel in his day and time, Luther performed this radical act daring to declare that the Church had gotten things wrong, and he wanted anyone who would read his theses to know it. Protestant Christians everywhere commemorate this day every year as Reformation Day and mark it as the beginning of the Protestant Church.

Can you imagine something like this happening to the North American Church? Picture it: An exasperated minister rushing up to the front entrances of some of the most popular megachurches in America and hanging up a statement listing all the teaching, doctrines, and practices their pastors and leaders have gotten wrong. Maybe it wouldn't be posted on their front doors or on a billboard. Maybe it would be a post on social media that goes viral throughout the metaverse and other virtual platforms.

Maybe we don't have to imagine this since it's happening all around us. Reports of misconduct, abuse of power, and misapplication of Scripture are making headlines every day. Can you imagine how the religious leaders of these churches may be angry and may want to silence the ones who have spoken up? This is just how it was for Martin Luther. While today we may assign merit to what he did, at the time his actions weren't celebrated. The Catholic Church wasn't too pleased with him.

In Matthew 23, we find Jesus doing the same thing. In His day, there were scribes and Pharisees who had begun to put forth practices that were not in line with God's law or agenda. Although they knew His law—they understood the letter of it down to a T—they were doing something completely different. In this chapter in Matthew, Jesus goes through a list of some of the things they would do—from always wanting the best seat in the house, to demanding that they be called by a certain title (see verses 1–12). Yet there was one action that caused Jesus to call them out. He said, "But woe to you, scribes and Pharisees, hypocrites! For you shut up the kingdom of heaven against men; for you neither go in yourselves, nor do you allow those who are entering to go in" (verse 13). Jesus spoke up for the people of God because these religious leaders had elevated themselves above the people they served and had begun to twist the words of God for their own benefit.

One of the important things to note about Jesus' time, and also Martin Luther's time, is that people didn't own their own personal Bibles, as we do today. Many were also illiterate. The way they came to know biblical truths and God's character was through what the priests, rabbis, or readers of the Scriptures read and interpreted for them. This is why the Bible says, "Be doers of the Word, and not hearers only" (James 1:22).

Because people weren't reading and studying for themselves, the perfect environment was created for wolves and false prophets to come in and twist the Gospel message and oppress them. From about the third century to the time of Martin Luther, it was a common occurrence for priests to sell "indulgences," as they were called. In other words, priests were charging people for the assurance that they would get into heaven. "If you want to be saved," the priests would say, "then you must pay this amount of money . . ." "If you want that healing to take place, then pay this amount . . ."

Unfortunately, we still see this kind of manipulation happening in the Church world today, and it's out of balance. It's not the will of God, nor is it sanctioned by Scripture. Jesus warned of this during His day. He said, "Beware of the false prophets, who come to you in sheep's clothing, but inwardly they are ravenous wolves" (Matthew 7:15). False prophets and wolves are religious leaders who manipulate the Word of God to bring greater influence and attention to themselves, keeping people dependent on them instead of on God, and twisting the Word to keep people in bondage. When they do this, Jesus said they "shut up the kingdom of heaven against men" (Matthew 23:13).

Or as one translation puts it, they "shut the door of the King-dom of Heaven in people's faces" (NLT). Another translation says they "lock up the kingdom of heaven from people" (HCSB). In other words, these religious oppressors set up strongholds that keep people from accessing the things they need from God and from heaven by teaching them false doctrines and requiring things from them that God never intended.

When Jesus used the phrase "kingdom of heaven" in this sense, He wasn't talking about entering into heaven when you die. He was talking about entering into heaven on earth, ex-periencing the Kingdom of God right here and now. Through religious oppression, the spirit of religion has tried to enter into our churches and ministries to shut down the move of God. It's very possible that due to this oppressive spirit, some of us are experiencing a plateau, limitation, or ceiling over our lives.

We sit under leaders who take the Scriptures and twist them, teaching us in error and suppressing an outpouring from heaven. Yet since we have access to the Scriptures and can now study for ourselves, how are we, in this modern era of the Church, finding ourselves shut out from heaven?

It may be that some of us were raised by people or were surrounded by abusive figures who constantly told us what we couldn't do: "You can't do this . . . You're not going to be able to succeed in that . . . You can't do this . . . That's not going to work for you . . ." If these words got into your spirit, then to this day your adult self—your thirty- or forty- or fifty-year-old self—is still fighting words that were said to you when you were perhaps just ten years old.

Because of this trauma, we may find ourselves in churches with leaders who echo some of the words we have heard and dysfunctional behaviors we have experienced from others. These leaders twist and manipulate the Word of the Lord, which affects our understanding of God. This in turn limits our access to the things of heaven.

Now it's easier to understand why the verse about faith coming by hearing is so significant: "So then faith comes by hearing, and hearing by the word of God" (Romans 10:17). When you hear error over and over again, you begin to believe it. And as the saying goes, "Your beliefs become your thoughts. Your thoughts become your words. Your words become your actions. Your actions become your habits. Your habits become your values. Your values become your destiny."[1]

You don't want your purposes and destiny impacted by error. What you hear matters. Social media and political entities understand this. That's why they're fighting for your attention with commercials, because it's not the truth that you will believe; it's what you hear the most that you will believe. Repetition embeds information in your subconscious, whether it's true or false.

This is why the enemy doesn't care if you only come to church on Sunday, because there are six other whole days out of the week when he can wage a war and fight to control what you hear—six of the days out of the week when demonic spirits fight for your attention and people fight for your ear. Everybody wants your ear. Everybody wants to convince you of something and get you to side with their beliefs. Therefore, you must guard your ears.

The people of Jesus' time and Martin Luther's time suffered because of ignorance and their lack of access to the Scriptures. The Bible says, "My people are destroyed for lack of knowledge" (Hosea 4:6). This applies in a lesser degree to believers in our day and time because many of us do have access to the Scriptures. No one can convince us without our being responsible at some level for what we believe, because we have personal access to the Bible. No one can convince us of a lie without our choosing to believe that lie. We can read and study for ourselves, and because of Jesus' ultimate sacrifice on the cross, we no longer need a priest to go before the Lord on our behalf.

Although we do need preachers so we can hear the Word, we can approach the throne of God boldly on our own as we seek His wisdom and provision (see Hebrews 4:16).

To break the bondage of religious oppression and resist the influence of leaders who have shut up the heavens over you, you must read and study the Word for yourself. As 2 Timothy 2:15 says, "Study to shew thyself approved unto God, a workman that needeth not to be ashamed, rightly dividing the word of truth" (KJV).

There is no excuse now for you to sit under oppressive religious teaching. You can combat false teachings and religious spirits with the truth of God's Word, which you know and are convinced of for yourself. To grow strong in the faith, read the Word, but don't just read it silently in your mind. Read it aloud, because then you'll be receiving it three times. Your eyes will see it, your mind will perceive it, and your ears will hear it.

The Word of God is truth, and the truth will set you free from religiously oppressive leaders' manipulation and influence. Make reading the Word aloud a regular practice, and you will begin to see a break in the bondage you've been under.

Next, repent for your part in leaving your spiritual growth in the hands of someone else. The Bible says we must each work out our own salvation with fear and trembling (see Philippians 2:12). The Holy Spirit, who leads us into all truth, dwells in us and abides with us, empowering us to know God's will and plan for our lives (see John 16:13). He is personally available to each of us. Ask Him, inquire of Him, and by His Spirit test everything you hear or are asked to do. But you must know Him and His voice first, so that it becomes the plumb line for everything else.

Then you'll want to renounce the hold on your life that you've given to ungodly leaders and false prophets—those who have spoken things over your life that have locked up your access to heaven. Recommit to giving God His rightful place as Lord over your life, and pray that He will surround you with righteous leaders, mentors, and friends whose teaching, prayers, and words will encourage you and help stir up the gift of God within you. As you are healed from the effects of various kinds of spiritually abusive relationships, pray that your discernment will be increased, and that you will know and cultivate authentic, godly connections and networks.

Finally, guard your ears. They are the gateway to your belief system. As you seek the Lord for breakthrough in this season where you are feeling as if you've hit a ceiling, ask yourself, *Who has been talking to me? Who has my ear? Whom have I been listening to? Whom have I been receiving from?*

Whoever it is, whatever you've been open to, whatever you hear the most, that's what you will believe and what will shape and influence how you are able to move in the assignment and purpose God has given you in this season.

Unconfessed, Unconfronted Sin

The ungodly spiritual leaders in your life can be one reason you are experiencing a closed heaven, or can be why you find yourself in a place where it seems as if things are locked up over you. Yet there is also the effect of unconfessed and unconfronted sin in our lives, or in our family line, which we call generational sin. First Kings 8:35–36 says this:

> When the heavens are shut up and there is no rain because they have sinned against You, when they pray toward this place and confess Your name, and turn from their sin because You afflict them, then hear in heaven, and forgive the sin of Your servants, Your people Israel, that You may teach them the good way in which they should walk; and send rain on Your land which You have given to Your people as an inheritance.

Our own sin is the one thing that separates us from God. Isaiah 59:2 (NLT) says, "It's your sins that have cut you off from God.

Because of your sins, he has turned away and will not listen anymore."

Sometimes, though, it isn't your own sin that has caused you to dwell under a closed heaven. It's possible that within your family, within your bloodline, there are those who have violated the principles of God. You can suffer because of someone else's violation (see Numbers 14:18).

Just as the heavens can be shut up due to sin, however, Scripture also shows that the heavens can be reopened because of repentance. In 2 Chronicles 7:13–14, which you may already be familiar with, God says,

> When I shut up heaven and there is no rain, or command the locusts to devour the land, or send pestilence among My people, if My people who are called by My name will humble themselves, and pray and seek My face, and turn from their wicked ways, then I will hear from heaven, and will forgive their sin and heal their land.

"If My people . . . turn from their wicked ways" simply means to repent. In essence, God is saying, *If My people would repent of sin . . .*

We don't have to be condemned by sin. We don't have to be stuck when we've been in sin. We don't have to get to a place where we're just so depressed because we've sinned. The only thing we need to do when we've sinned is *turn*. God says, *If you do that, I will hear from heaven and will heal your land.*

Let's look at the words *land* and *earth* as they are used in these verses we've been talking about. Remember Deuteronomy 28:23 (KJV): "And thy heaven that is over thy head shall be brass, and the earth that is under thee shall be iron." That use of *earth* is connected to the reason why God said He was going to heal the *land* in 2 Chronicles 7:14, because when the heavens are shut up, it affects your land—not just the natural earth, either.

It also affects *you* because you come from the dust of the earth. You and I are connected to the earth. Revelation 12:16 tells us this as well. The earth that opened its mouth and swallowed up the water that spewed out against the woman represents the Church. The earth was literally helping the woman. This symbolism shows that we are connected to the earth.

Anytime the heavens are shut up over you, or you feel as if you've gotten to a place where things are closed, it automatically will affect the earth beneath you. In other words, when the Bible talks about the earth—and I want you to hear this word I'm giving—it's also referring to you. At the beginning, when God made humankind, He made us from the dust of the earth (see Genesis 2:7). When the heavens are shut up, then the earth is also closed up—that's you and me. Therefore, like barren and parched land, you will yield no fruit.

But when you repent from your sin and the sins committed by those in your family line, renouncing the power of sin in your life, and when you pray and seek the face of God, He will forgive you, heal you, and break the ceiling over your life. You will once again sit under an open heaven.

When the Heavens Open

Get ready to see the shattering of a ceiling. That's what God told me as I sought Him in prayer when I felt as though I had hit a plateau in my life. He started by teaching me how to break through when it feels as if every opportunity is locked and when you pray, nothing happens. He gave me greater understanding of what was happening in that kind of scenario. He also gave me a strategy on how to come out of that place. Then He told me to share with you all He has shared with me. He wants you to know that as you realign with Him by breaking the influence of ungodly leadership and repenting of any sin in your life or in your family line, you will experience an opening in the heavens. The ceiling that has been above your head in the spirit is about to break open. You're about to see that brass ceiling shatter.

What does this mean? This means that within your community, within your city, within your region, within your career field, within the industry the Lord has placed you in, you will experience a release from all that was capping you. You will emerge at a whole new level. You will come into another dimension and see four specific things happen: (1) *you gain access to revelation*, (2) *limitations are shattered*, (3) *the bar is raised*, and (4) *you become a bloodline breaker*. Let's look at each of these now.

1. You gain access to revelation.

When the Lord opens the heavens over you, He gives you access to revelation—or revealed knowledge—and the wisdom to carry out what He reveals. This revelation was there the whole time, but it was hidden in plain sight as you sat under a closed heaven.

The revelation God gives you access to reveals the wisdom and knowledge hidden in Christ. You cannot get access to those while blinded by spiritual deception and sin (your own sin or the sins in your family line). You cannot be under the control of mankind or the flesh and gain access to the things of God.

We have the opportunity to engage in two levels of knowledge. One is natural knowledge—the knowledge we learn in school or what we experience through our five senses. The other is revealed knowledge—the kind that can only come from the Spirit of God. As 1 Corinthians 2:12–14 says,

> Now we have received, not the spirit of the world, but the Spirit who is from God, that we might know the things that have been freely given to us by God.

These things we also speak, not in words which man's wisdom teaches but which the Holy Spirit teaches, comparing spiritual things with spiritual. But the natural man does not receive the things of the Spirit of God, for they are foolishness to him; nor can he know them, because they are spiritually discerned.

I began to pray this through, and God said, *There are things I'm about to do in your life. There are things I will do for you that will require a dimension of wisdom you do not currently have. What I am doing in your life will require access to knowledge and information.*

As God breaks the ceiling over your life, you will enter a time when the words He has spoken will be performed at an accelerated pace. There will also be unusual releases from the Spirit of God, but these things are only going to come through the gateway of wisdom. This means you will need to pray more for wisdom than you have prayed for it in the past, because the only thing separating you from the next season, the new chapter in your life, is simply knowledge and wisdom.

Wisdom unlocks doors. Wisdom leads you down avenues you didn't even know were there. With wisdom, you'll be able to then take possession of the territory God has ordained for you. When Solomon was given an opportunity to ask the Lord for anything, he could have asked for money, but he didn't. He could have asked for great riches and treasures, but no. The Lord came to him in a dream and said, "Ask! What shall I give you?" (1 Kings 3:5). The Bible tells us that Solomon asked the Lord for wisdom, a discerning heart, and to know how to go in and amongst the people. God answered him,

Because you have asked this thing, and have not asked long life for yourself, nor have asked riches for yourself, nor have asked the life of your enemies, but have asked for yourself understanding to discern justice, behold, I have done according to your words; see, I have given you a wise and understanding heart, so that there has not been anyone like you before you, nor shall any like you arise after you. And I have also given you what you have not asked: both riches and honor, so that there shall not be anyone like you among the kings all your days.

1 Kings 3:11–13

There is something that gets God's attention: when we come to Him in faith, asking Him for wisdom. As James 1:5 tells us, He will give it to us without limit. I'm sharing this with you because the ceiling that once capped and limited your mind and your movement is about to break. As you turn away from what was binding you and toward God, who sets you free, you will receive revelation knowledge and divine information that you didn't have.

Instead of praying and asking the Lord simply for provision for a day, you will have the wisdom to ask Him for a strategy so that you never return to the place of poverty you were in. You will pray, *Lord, give me wisdom to navigate my future and to deal with this industry You put me in. Give me wisdom to deal with people and relationships.*

When we ask the Lord for wisdom, He will download it to us. Many times, we think we need great faith to keep that mega dream or vision God has placed within us working. But the Bible tells us that people perish for lack of knowledge, not lack of faith (see Hosea 4:6). Listen, faith is important, and it's impossible to please God without faith (see Hebrews 11:6). But people are not perishing and their dreams are not dying for lack of faith. They are perishing for lack of knowledge.

I believe that many people have great faith. As a matter of fact, we know from Romans 12:3 that God has given a measure of faith to everybody. But what most of us have failed to do is add wisdom and knowledge to the faith we have. We can pray and push all day, but then there's no movement after we have prayed. We can fast and consecrate ourselves to God, but then after we have finished fasting, there are no actions we put into practice, no wisdom applied. There's no movement behind what you believe. But when the ceiling breaks, what has been hiding in plain sight—the information you need to get to the next level—is uncovered. Revelation brings what is hidden to light.

2. Limitations are shattered.

The second thing that happens when the heavens open is that limitations are shattered. Where you've run into barriers, where you've been pushing and getting nowhere, God says, *I'm removing that limitation.*

3. The bar is raised.

As the heavens open over your life, there are certain benchmarks you will push into. You will reach levels and places you've never reached before. You will now hit new goals in your life and for your family that you've not reached before. You will be the opener and the trailblazer for those who are coming behind you. The bar is being raised.

4. You become a bloodline breaker.

Finally, whatever generational curse was on your bloodline and on your family, whether it was a curse of sickness and infirmity or something else, it has to break when the heavens open over you. If it was a curse of poverty, you're going to see it break off not just you, but also off your family.

When the heavens open, things must change. I prophetically declare over you that you're in a season where you are about to see God open up the heavens for you, and you're going to receive a download, whether it's for your family, your ministry, your life, your business, or your career. The Lord will give you new insight.

MANTLE MOMENT

For the next thirty seconds, I want you to think of something you don't currently know. Let your thoughts and concerns about it rise to the surface. Pray this:

Lord, what do I need to know that I don't know? You put me in this place, this area, and I need to learn this specific thing, but I don't know how to do it yet. Lord, You gave me an idea, but I don't know how to take it from this stage to the next one.

With this thing in your mind and heart, I invite you to pray with me. As we discussed in this chapter, it's important to ask God for wisdom. You need the know-how to do what God has asked of you, the know-how to be successful in the area He has called you to. James 1:5 says, "If any of you lacks wisdom, let him ask of God, who gives to all liberally," and God will not hold it back from you. Let's pray this prayer now:

Father, give me the wisdom, the know-how to go in and amongst the people. Show me how to govern. Give me the wisdom to guide those You have put into my care. Like Solomon, I don't ask for money; I ask You for wisdom.
  —Give me the wisdom to care for and raise my family.
  —Give me the wisdom to cover my spouse.
  —Give me the wisdom to nurture my children.
  —Give me the wisdom to prosper in my business.
  —Give me the wisdom to see daily provision.
  —Give me the wisdom to generate ideas.
  —Give me the wisdom and knowledge to win souls.
  —Give me the wisdom and knowledge to be a distributor of resources to others.

Lord, I ask for wisdom to be a gatekeeper and a door opener for those who come behind. Let me become a lender and not a borrower. Give me the wisdom to lead, and give me a Joseph anointing to house what you've given me to house.

Father, I pray for wisdom now, in Jesus' name, Amen.

7

MANTLED TO BREAK CURSES

You know how we exhorted, and comforted, and charged every one of you, as a father does his own children . . .

1 Thessalonians 2:11

I grew up in a Christian household, which jumpstarted my journey in learning the character traits it takes to serve others. My parents were both pastors, and I learned early on about the challenges and the rewards of ministry. First, the challenges of ministry made me want to run from any form of publicly serving within the Church. I watched my parents and my other pastors endure tests of betrayal, extreme warfare, and financial hardship, all for the sake of a cause they were willing to suffer for.

It would be some years later that I would even begin to understand the true value of faith in Jesus Christ. As I developed a deep, personal relationship with the Lord, I grew to understand that suffering for something or someone you love is actually an honor. That was the moment my eyes opened up to see the beautiful reward of serving in ministry. I looked beyond the challenges, to see the countless lives impacted by the message of the Gospel. I discovered the reward of seeing broken people healed, rejected people accepted into the family of Christ, and lost people found, receiving their God-given identity. The reward of serving is priceless. The quality of being a servant is the key to being fulfilled in life.

Years later, I found myself engulfed in the study of Elijah and Elisha. This spiritual father-son relationship intrigued me. It models a dynamic and a depth of relationship showing two generations merging together to fulfill a God-given assignment in the earth. This is powerful! These kinds of relationships are even more important now because of the enemy's assault against families, including both natural and spiritual children and parents. The enemy has waged warfare against multigenerations coming together, because he knows that there's power and impact in those alignments. I believe that God is releasing the spirit of Elijah to restore fractured families and to heal a rift in the Body of Christ between generations. We will truly see the hearts of fathers turn toward sons, and the hearts of sons turn toward fathers.

Over a decade ago, I found myself in one of the most vulnerable and broken places of my life. I was traveling around the country, preaching and ministering to others, but my life and the world as I knew it was falling apart. Someone whom I had looked up to in ministry for years went spiraling down into a destructive pattern due to unhealed soul wounds. Ministries were displaced, relationships were broken, and people were hurting. Of course, the Lord didn't cause this situation, but He allowed it and used it for my good (see Romans 8:28). Myriad questions raced through my mind as a result: *How could this have happened? Why won't this person humble himself/herself and get help? Where does this leave me?* I went into a period of consecration, fasting, and prayer. After several months, the

Lord spoke to me and said, *I had to allow your world to fall apart because I'm bringing you into a new world.*

I thought, *What does this mean?*

God said to me, *The spiritual place that you have been in is not conducive for where I'm taking you. I'm sending you a father who will pour into you, correct you, and prepare you for your purpose.*

It was at that time, when I was the most broken, that a spiritual father—my Elijah—entered my life. And the journey began.

Finding Identity

As an Elisha, the greatest lesson I have learned is that I didn't know who I was. I thought I knew who I was, but I had no clue. I had taken on fragments of who people wanted me to be and what I thought people would like, and I had hidden behind a cloak disguised as my personality. There are negative bloodline issues that emerge when you aren't walking in your identity in Christ. In biology it's known as *epigenetics*, which is "the study of the chemical modification of specific genes or gene-associated proteins of an organism. Epigenetic modifications can define how the information in genes is expressed and used by cells."[1]

In other words, epigenetics is a pattern or gene sequence placed on top of one's DNA (*epi* means "on top of"). Studies have shown that what a person's ancestors have experienced is hidden within the DNA of the generations that come after them. For instance, if a group of people has gone through trauma, it can manifest in a descendant's DNA without him or her ever having experienced the same trauma. Experts have compared these markers in the DNA to flipping on a switch. Epigenetics studies show that the wrong environment can bring out these triggers or markers within the blood. For example, an unstable environment can trigger a mental disorder that was lying dormant, or a fear-filled environment can trigger an autoimmune disease.

A study conducted in 2015 by Rachel Yehuda and her team at the Icahn School of Medicine at Mount Sinai in New York City published results from observing the descendants of Holocaust survivors.[2] These Holocaust survivors had either been interned in Nazi concentration camps or had been forced into hiding during World War II. They were exposed to torture and immense trauma. After it was over, however, they went on to live their lives. But the study focused on their descendants. Although their descendants weren't exposed to torture or trauma, invisible markers were found that altered a gene linked to their levels of cortisol. The results are controversial and are disputed by some. However, the study found that the offspring of those Holocaust survivors were predisposed to anxiety disorders. By understanding this from a natural, scientific perspective, we can relate it to the spiritual. Experiences, as well as deeds done by previous generations, can pass down in a bloodline. Deuteronomy 5:9 explains that the iniquity of the fathers can manifest itself up to the third and fourth generations.

The good news is that Jesus Christ broke the curse, blotted out the iniquity, destroyed the yoke, and severed the bondage the enemy puts us in. But it is only through receiving the Spirit of adoption that we fully experience this freedom (see Romans 8:15). The Lord has raised up fathers and mothers in the faith to point the way to freedom. They have the ability to change the spiritual gene sequence in order to push sons and daughters into divine purpose. They are called to nurture, correct, and instruct us so we can become more like Christ.

Through biblical spiritual fathering, bloodline curses are broken and you receive the identity of the heavenly Father. The word *father* in the New Testament is the Greek word *patér*.[3] It's where we get the English word *pattern* from. Spiritual fathers and mothers are patterns. They chart paths, take spiritual hits, and pioneer spiritual territory so that we can walk through unhindered. The apostle Paul often spoke of his assignment as a spiritual father. In Galatians 4:19 (ESV) he wrote of "my little children, for whom I am again in the anguish of childbirth until Christ is formed in you!" He described his experience as birthing those who were accountable to his ministry until Christ was formed in them.

As an Elisha, I have learned the need for spiritual parenting on this level. In Scripture, God used Elijah to imprint His anointing and will on the heart and life of Elisha. Through Elijah fathering Elisha, God superimposed His DNA into Elisha's life. Likewise, God used my spiritual father to help me rediscover my true identity in Christ. My spiritual father has pointed me to Christ, and has taught me biblical principles and the need for accountability. I have had the privilege of traveling with him and ministering together in conferences and church services. Identity is truly found in the coming together of the generations. There is no son without a father. When the hearts of fathers and sons unite, we will carry a deeper and more clear reflection of the image of Christ.

The Need for Accountability

One of the most memorable phrases my spiritual father spoke to me is "the greater the gift, the greater the need for accountability." Being accountable is submitting one's actions and decisions to be inspected or properly judged by someone else. Accountability is a safeguard—a protective measure for the one who chooses it. There are several benefits of an Elisha being accountable to an Elijah:

1. Accountability develops character.
2. Accountability provides a hedge of protection.
3. Accountability unlocks wisdom.

4. Accountability brings clarity and eradicates confusion.

5. Accountability fosters growth.

6. Accountability positions you to receive impartation.

7. Accountability releases God's favor upon your life.

Submission is required in order to be accountable to a spiritual leader. Unfortunately, we are in a generation that has been abused, mishandled, and even spiritually assaulted under the guise of submission. The enemy has fueled this twisting of spiritual authority in order to cause people to back away from pure and true submission to proper spiritual authority. I believe that in the coming days, we will see a wave of inner healing come to a generation that has been rejected, abandoned, and mistreated. The Lord is raising up those who truly have His heart to pour into others.

Submission is a beautiful thing if done the biblical way. Submission means the action or fact of accepting or yielding to a superior force, or to the will or authority of another person.[4] Submission is an act of the will. When Jesus was in the Garden of Gethsemane, He was teaching us submission to the Father. Although in the flesh He wanted the bitter cup He must drink to pass from Him, He knew it was the Father's will that He drink of that cup. He therefore spoke those famous words "not My will, but Yours, be done" (Luke 22:42).

As spiritual sons and daughters, we must learn that we are here to carry out the will of the Father. He has ordained spiritual authority, but we must freely and willingly submit to it. Spiritual authority is the compass that will help guide us during tough times. It is a beacon of light in the darkness.

Positioned for Impartation

My spiritual father was in a service in Houston, teaching and ministering under a heavy anointing. This was a couple of years after he became my spiritual father, and I flew in from Minneapolis just for this event. The Lord had placed it on my heart that there was an impartation for me. Several people I knew were at the service. They pastored churches in various cities. As the service ended, I was standing in the sanctuary with a group of people, talking and laughing. I was really enjoying the fellowship and the Word that had come forth. Immediately, my spiritual father walked up to me in front of a room full of people and proceeded to ask me a list of questions. He used a very authoritative tone, and the questions seemed personal. He started by saying, "I need an account of what's going on in your life and ministry. If I am your spiritual father, then I have the right to ask concerning your character, actions, and decisions."

Standing there in front of other pastors and leaders, I had to give an open account of my personal and ministry details. Then he abruptly said, "I need to see you after the next service."

Honestly, I was embarrassed. It seemed as though I were in trouble and had done something wrong. I sat through the next service nervous about what the meeting might entail. But I pressed through to worship and to receive the Word. After the service, I tracked my spiritual father down privately. He then began to correct me in some areas of my personal life. I humbled myself to receive because I knew this was the Lord. The undertone of his voice was infused with love. Although the things he was saying were stern, the love of Christ was there. He told me, "The Lord said to me that I need to spend more time pouring into you. Every Tuesday, we will talk. I will share the Word with you and impart to you."

This started a journey of impartation through the teaching of the Word. Those Tuesday sessions went on for some years. Although I was pastoring a growing church and ministering around the country and abroad, I had a pastor who was teaching me each week. Today, the times and days have changed, but I still receive teaching and impartation. I value those times of impartation even more now. The words my spiritual father personally shared with me have healed brokenness in my soul, built my faith, empowered me to step out on the instructions God gave me, and helped me avoid pitfalls. Through this experience with my spiritual father, I've learned that you must be positioned to receive impartation. It's not about a natural positioning, but a posture of the heart. Further, I've learned the necessity of being poured into. I had gone years pouring into others and had not consistently been poured into. I could feel my spirit being strengthened as he did this for me. I was being equipped for the work of the ministry. Even more importantly than that, my soul was being cared for and pastored.

I find that some people only want the gift of another person. They want the performance, the skill, or the talent of an individual, but they don't care about the soul of that person. True Elijahs place the person before his or her gift. Our character and who we are is more important than how well we can perform. It is only when placing people ahead of their gift that you come to realize that people are the real gifts. Walking alongside my spiritual father has shown me that God loved me enough to send me help. God loves me so much that He would instruct and teach me, using someone (my spiritual father) to correct me in love.

In addition, an Elijah carries a depth of wisdom that is needed in an Elisha. Throughout my journey, I have found that wisdom is essential. You cannot rely on your talent to navigate the difficulties of life and ministry. It requires experience, wisdom, and knowledge. As the Lord is merging the generations, a fusion of wisdom and strength is taking place. Job 12:12 (csb) says, "Wisdom is found with the elderly, and understanding comes with long life." We need the wisdom of the older generation. They know the path that we should take.

Furthermore, 1 John 2:14 says, "I have written to you, young men, because you are strong." The young generation has a strength and stamina that only come with youth. When the two generations come together and combine strength and wisdom, we are unstoppable against the plans and plots of the devil. Our Christian faith is generational. The blessing of God is generational. Our God is a God of generations! With that being said, I am excited to be an Elisha running with the Elijah God has assigned me to.

MANTLE MOMENT

You have been mantled to break curses! Through the power of Jesus Christ, you have already overcome any bondage the enemy would try to place upon you. Now, you have to walk in the finished work of Christ by applying biblical principles to your life in order to see the results that you're believing, speaking, and declaring. In this chapter, I shared the need for having a mentor, a spiritual father or mother. However, when having a mentor isn't possible, God uses processes, trials, and life to train and teach you. If you are looking for a mentor, what kind of leader are you looking for to be a godly example in your life? I also listed seven benefits of accountability. How will you commit to being more accountable so that these benefits will apply to you?

8

MANTLED FOR MIRACLES

He replied, "What is impossible with man is possible with God."

Luke 18:27 csb

I believe that the working of miracles is one of the most needed teachings when it comes to believers. When we look at evangelists throughout the New Testament, an interesting theme emerges of them operating in the gifts of the Spirit within their evangelistic calling. Whether it be with Stephen or one of the several other evangelists, you see this theme repeated. We see that the working of miracles is a gift given to evangelists.

Any believer can operate in the working of miracles, but we regularly see this gift coupled together with soul winning. The Lord would use an evangelist to win souls by the gift of miracles because this gift shows a sign to those who don't believe. There are those who sometimes need a sign to get their attention and give them confirmation that God is real and that

He exists. Look at the life of Jesus Christ as He was carrying out His assignment in the flesh on the earth. The Bible says He healed many who were sick or oppressed, and they followed Him and believed on Him. Others would see these signs of the healing or miracle that took place and know that God was with Jesus as He walked the earth. Of course, we know that there are lying signs and wonders as well. Yet if there are lying signs and wonders, that means there has to be something that is a real sign and wonder—authentic, a miracle that is actually real that the Lord has given to the believer.

You may be reading this and be among those who still don't know if miracles are for today. I want to bring your attention to 1 Corinthians 14:12, which says, "Even so you, since you are zealous for spiritual gifts, let it be for the edification of the church that you seek to excel." The apostle Paul is saying that it's okay for us to want spiritual gifts. It's actually a good thing for us to seek spiritual gifts so we might edify the Church. That's one aspect of a spiritual gift. But then we also understand that the Lord would often use miracles in the New Testament to get the attention of those who didn't believe. So there's a dual function of miracles in edifying the Church. First, they build the faith of the Church, of those who already believe. Second, they get the attention of those who don't believe, and they bring those people to the door of salvation.

It's important to study 1 Corinthians 12:10 because it gives us insight and understanding into how some of this works. It's important to study and understand how the gift of miracles works. This verse talks about the distribution of gifts and how God gives "to another the working of miracles, to another prophecy, to another discerning of spirits . . ." We want to focus on the fact that it says to another, God gives the working of miracles. And then also focus on the way verse 11 says, "But one and the same Spirit works all these things, distributing to each one individually as He wills." It all happens according to how

God intends for the gifts to be distributed. Everybody doesn't receive the same spiritual gifts, which is why you can seek after other gifts, including the working of miracles.

I believe if you're a Christian, you should be hungry to operate in the gifts of the Spirit. I believe you shouldn't just be satisfied with mere words, and you shouldn't just be satisfied with giving a mere message, without the demonstration of that message through signs and wonders. This is very biblical because we see evangelists in Scripture who operate in miracles. This is one of the ways they flow in their ministries, and many nonbelievers came into the Kingdom because of miracles that broke out in Scripture.

You Have to Want It!

I've also seen this in operation in modern times today, so I want to take a deep look at it. When we're talking about the working of miracles, we need to look at how to activate them in our lives as believers and as evangelists. First, if you're going to be used of God, *you have to want it!* The first thing is wanting it. You have to want to operate in miracles.

I know that the religiously oppressive Church has told you that you shouldn't want those things and has told you not to go after them. And no, we don't chase signs and wonders. But there's nothing wrong with wanting the Holy Spirit to use you as a vessel, as a conduit to bring about miracles in the lives of other people to help them. So you do need to want it. If you don't seek for the Holy Spirit to use you in this way, then you won't see some of the miracles and signs that you could see. I want to give you permission right now to seek spiritual gifts. This is what Paul told the New Testament Church, and that message is still for us today—that you have permission to seek after spiritual gifts. You have permission to pursue them, as long as your motive is edifying others.

As long as your motive is edifying the Church and winning lost souls, then seek after spiritual gifts. You can actually pray for the Lord to use you in this way. You can say, *Lord, use me as a vessel to produce miracles in the earth, and You will get all the glory!*

Why not you? That's the question. Why not you, now? I know this may go against the way some people have been taught, but I want you to understand that those of us whom the Lord has used and does use in miracles, we *want* it. We want to see the Holy Spirit break out among His people. We want to see the Holy Spirit heal people and do what is impossible.

Every Miracle Was a Lesson

Now that we know we must want a miracle, let's talk about what a miracle is. In our English language, a *miracle* can be defined as something that occurs that is humanly impossible, or something that defies or contradicts natural laws. The first recorded miracle of Jesus was when He turned water into wine. That was a powerful miracle because it defied natural laws. It is impossible in our human state for us to take water and get wine out of it. None of us should be able to do this. The only way something like that can occur is by the God of Israel, the God of wonders, by our God whom we serve.

Every miracle Jesus performed was a lesson. This is something the Holy Spirit began teaching me that I want to share with you. Jesus never performed a miracle just to perform it. Yes, if it was a miraculous healing, it was done to heal that person. Yet it had greater implications for those who were watching. Whether it was a healing or any other miracle, there was something to be taught from it.

Look at the first miracle Jesus performed, or at least the first that is recorded. John 2:1–4 says,

On the third day there was a wedding in Cana of Galilee, and the mother of Jesus was there. Now both Jesus and His disciples were invited to the wedding. And when they ran out of wine, the mother of Jesus said to Him, "They have no wine."

Jesus said to her, "Woman, what does your concern have to do with Me? My hour has not yet come."

If we look deeper into the communication between Jesus and His mother, we can surmise that He probably had performed miracles that may not have been public, so they may not have been recorded. It is evident that His mother knew He could perform miracles. She knew He was the Christ, the anointed one, and she knew He was God in the flesh. And Jesus submitted Himself to the authority of His earthly parents.

We see this submission back in the biblical account where Mary and Joseph couldn't find Jesus for three days when He was twelve years old, and they were panicking. They eventually found Him teaching in the Temple, and He said, "Did you not know that I must be about my father's business?" (Luke 2:49). And the Bible says that from that day forward, Jesus obeyed them or submitted Himself to them (see verse 51). That was an example and sign of Jesus, God in the flesh, submitting to His parents' natural authority. This miracle of turning water into wine has a lesson in it—that it's likewise key that as an evangelist, you have to know the power in submitting to spiritual authority under someone else.

Mary and Joseph were an apostolic type; they give us a leadership model where someone anointed, Jesus, was submitting to natural authority. And they show us that whomever you are submitted to spiritually has the ability to accelerate your time. Even though in effect Jesus said to His mother, *Woman, it's not My time. What have I to do with you?*, He still complied with and obeyed her request. In fact, according to what's written, she didn't even respond to what He said.

Instead, she said to the servants, "Whatever He says to you, do it" (John 2:5).

It's interesting that His mother didn't even respond to what Jesus was saying about the timing, because she operated in that level of authority. Because she had the authority to activate His time, she was able to turn to the servants and tell them how they would be used to activate this miracle. Verses 6–10 tell us the rest of the story:

> Now there were set there six waterpots of stone, according to the manner of purification of the Jews, containing twenty or thirty gallons apiece. Jesus said to them, "Fill the waterpots with water." And they filled them up to the brim. And He said to them, "Draw some out now, and take it to the master of the feast." And they took it. When the master of the feast had tasted the water that was made wine, and did not know where it came from (but the servants who had drawn the water knew), the master of the feast called the bridegroom. And he said to him, "Every man at the beginning sets out the good wine, and when the guests have well drunk, then the inferior. You have kept the good wine until now!"

There are some powerful lessons in this miracle that I want us to unpack. First, *every miracle requires preparation.* Second, *every miracle has to be activated.* Third, *you must work your gift.* And fourth, *in order to operate, it's going to take faith.* With Jesus as our example, let me explain what I mean by each of these.

Every miracle requires preparation.

Jesus performed a miracle, and every miracle is performed by a set of actions. Every miracle therefore takes preparation. If you want to see miracles in your life, you will have to prepare for them. If you're going to be used of God to perform miracles, you need preparation. For every miracle, there's a set of instructions that must be followed. God never does a miracle without some kind of instructions being followed. Even if they only involve the person performing the miracle or praying, there will be preparation. Sometimes, that preparation involves you praying and fasting. There are times where you will have to pray and you will have to fast and believe God in your own personal time, before you publicly begin praying for miracles for someone else. There's always preparation involved.

The Bible says there were six waterpots, and Jesus' mother tells the servants to do whatever Jesus says. These six stone pots were sitting there, and Jesus instructs the servants to go and get them. The pots were huge, and when you study this, you find that each held gallons of liquid. They weren't small pots, but huge ones used for purification. After the servants bring the stone pots, Jesus tells them to now fill them up with water. Here is the practical or the natural, before we see the super. We talk about the supernatural, but many times we don't understand that there has to be the natural first. There are things that must be done in the natural before God begins to sovereignly move.

There are also times where the Holy Spirit can intervene and just do things on His own. But when He's using us as vessels in the earth, there is a natural assignment for us to do first. These servants have now been activated to assist, and they actually have to get the stone waterpots, fill them up with water, and then draw it out. You may have noticed that they aren't given a whole lot of detailed instruction, but it was enough. If they hadn't gotten the stone pots, and if they hadn't filled them up with water, then no miracle would have been produced. It's important as you're operating in your evangelistic call that when God begins to push you to administer miracles and healing in the lives of others, you listen for His small instructions and pay attention to the small thing or things the Lord is telling you to do.

Every miracle has to be activated.

I remember one of the first notable miracles that God used me for was when I had a person's deaf ear open in a service I was doing. This was new to me at the time. I had never operated quite in that way, but the Lord was pushing me into a place of miracles. Since that time, I've seen so many different types of miracles that have happened as a result of the Holy Spirit using me. Of course, He gets all the glory for it! We don't take glory for any of God's works. We know that it's Him, and He uses us. And as I said before, there are things we must do to prepare. In this particular instance, the Lord gave me instructions as I was ministering a message in a morning session. Somewhere in the middle of my message, I heard the Lord say to me that He wanted to perform miracles. He told me to prophesy, *There is a miracle anointing entering in this service, and God is about to perform miracles.*

Here you can see the gifts working together. Just by a word of knowledge I was told that the gift of miracles and working of miracles was about to happen. And the word of knowledge works with the other eight spiritual gifts. There are nine in total, but it works in conjunction with the other gifts. The Lord gave me a word of knowledge that somebody deaf in one ear was in the room. I had never done this before, but I called the person out who fit what the Lord described. I told the crowd that I had heard the Lord say there's somebody deaf here, and I called for the person to come forward. A woman came up. Again, I had never done this before, so I was in shock at this point and I began praying, *Lord, okay, what am I supposed to do? I know how to pray, and I know how to command by Your Word, to speak what You say. I know how to decree, but what do You want me to do?*

The Lord told me to do something that seemed odd to me. I hadn't done this before, although now it's a very common-place occurrence. I'm sure many who operate in the working of miracles have been prompted to operate in the same way. The Lord told me to get some oil, and He said, *I want you to dip your finger in the oil and then put it in the ear of this person.*

I called for somebody to bring the oil very quickly. They brought me whatever anointing oil they could find, and I put my finger in the oil and told the people what I was about to do. I dipped my finger in the oil and put it into the ear of the deaf person, and then I prayed. Now, those were simple instructions I was following, but a miracle has to be activated. You need to find out what you need to do to activate that gift, for this moment, for now. There are times that the gift is inside you but not always active. It's not always working, so you have to learn how to activate the miracle.

After I prayed, as soon as I took my finger out of the person's ear she started screaming and saying that she could hear now. I'm going to be honest with you—I was just as shocked as she was. I had never been used of God to do anything like this. Back then this was new to me; this was different. The Lord was just beginning to bring me into a ministry of healing and miracles, so I was just as shocked as the healed person was, and I started rejoicing with her. But I was also thinking, *O, my God, You just did this!*

Then praise began to erupt, and the faith of the people in that church began to shoot through the roof. I'm talking about real faith shooting through the roof! Then by virtue of this miracle taking place, other miracles begin to happen, other breakthroughs within the service. Other people experienced encounters with Jesus, all because one miracle began to shake that place. I'm telling you this because when you're operating in the working of miracles, you must learn to activate that gift within you in order to move in the gift of miracles.

You must work your gift.

Let's talk about what it means to work your gift. We just learned that you have to activate your gift, but this is a different category. You also have to work that gift. You must understand that this is why the Bible calls it *the working of miracles*. You can see this in 1 Corinthians 12:10, and it's interesting phraseology that you don't see very often in the New Testament. It doesn't say *miracles* or even *the gift of miracles*. It says *the working of miracles*. Language is important, so let's look at what the word *working* really means in the original language. We have to understand that when we're reading the Scriptures, we're reading ancient manuscripts, and language has evolved over thousands of years. Not only are you talking about language evolving from year to year, but you're also talking about multiple translations of Scripture. So going back to the original language brings us a clearer understanding of what we're reading.

We know that the Old Testament was written in Hebrew and the New Testament was written in Greek, with some small portions in Aramaic. Sometimes you have to go to the original language to see the Hebrew, Greek, or Aramaic meaning of a word or phrase. Otherwise, there is nuance in language that we can sometimes easily miss. Think about how everyone talked in your town or city where you grew up. Think about how you talked amongst your friends and family. Now think about how differently you talk now. Think about how some words have different meanings even from ten years ago. With Scripture we are going back thousands of years, and we can't do that without considering how language has evolved and how these ancient words have been translated. Sometimes things can be lost in translation. This is why we study the Word. My prayer is that as you are reading this, it ignites in you a hunger to study the Word. The more you study the Word, the more it becomes alive in your spirit.

In the working of miracles, the Greek word for *working* is *energēma*, and it means an effect that is operating and working.[1] But if we look at the root word, *energeō*, it means to be active, to be efficient, to be mighty in, to show forth itself, and to work effectively.[2] Let's keep digging deeper and go to the root word for *energeō*. We are backtracking until we get to the etymology of the word *working*. The root of the word for *energeō* is *energēs*, and this means active, operative, effectual, and powerful.[3] So the word literally means working, but it also means active. This tells us the Scripture is saying *active miracles*. To some, God gives the working or the activation—the effectiveness of miracles. We now know that *working* is dealing with activating, using, or operating in that particular gift. God gives us the operation of miracles.

This is powerful because we need to understand that there are multiple operations to miracles. The word *working* means "operations" plural, meaning there are different vehicles that the Holy Spirit uses to bring forth miracles. Some miracles come through prayer, some through fasting, some through simple faith being stirred up in a room. Some are released through a person releasing his or her testimony. Once a testimony is released, that kind of miracle also happens for someone else in the room. Some miracles come from a place of worship, and God just moves sovereignly. Some miracles come by a seed that is sown. I remember an instance where I was believing God for a release of a mega amount of money, and it was going to take a miracle to get it. The Lord told me to sow a seed. I sowed the seed, as the Lord instructed me, and it hurt to sow it, but it broke open the miracle.

When you're in a situation that needs a miracle, you must ask the Holy Spirit, *What vehicle, what method, what operation do You want to use to bring about the miracle?* Not all operations work for every situation. I was ministering to a woman who needed to be healed, and her family thought she was going to die. The family came to me after a service and begged me to come to the hospital where she was. They said the doctors had given up, and they didn't know what to do. She couldn't walk, she didn't have any strength, she couldn't even sit up in bed on her own, and she was dealing with about nine different ailments and diseases. Some of the family approached me at the hospital and said they had also done all they could do. They said they had prayed, had fasted for weeks, and had believed God. They said they believed that she wasn't being healed because she didn't want to be.

When I arrived in this woman's hospital room, the staff made me put on a mask. This was several years before the pandemic, and masks weren't used in our general population at the time. They asked me to put on a mask and gloves because of whatever ailments and diseases this woman was fighting, so I put them on. When I got in the room, I saw the spirit of death sitting on her, and the Lord told me how to pray. Remember that every miracle takes a certain operation for it to come to pass. There was no seed that needed to be sown here; that's a different kind of situation. Typically, the vehicle for the situation is going to correlate to the type of miracle you need. If I would have gone and sown a seed to my pastor for the woman's healing, it wouldn't have worked in that situation.

This time, the Lord told me to lay hands on the woman and command the spirit of infirmity and death to leave her body. I laid my hands on her and commanded exactly that. I cast the spirit out of her by the name of Jesus Christ, and it left her. Then I told her that she needed worship music playing in her room.

The doctors also had told her she would never walk again. They said if she did come out of her illness, it would be six months before she walked, and she would have to go into therapy to learn to walk again first. Literally the next day, within 24 hours after I had prayed, she was up walking and doing what she and the doctors had said she couldn't do. The Lord brought her out of it and healed her body completely. Her family sent word to me that God had raised her up, and it was because of the miracle-working power that was released the day I was sent to the hospital. Of course, God gets all the glory for it. It was such a powerful miracle that the woman was featured in a magazine for what the Lord had done in her life, and God did get all the glory!

I'm sharing this to show you that there are different operations for miracles. Sometimes a spirit needs to be cast out, and you need to talk to the Holy Spirit and discern if that's the situation you are facing. In the above situation I had to cast the spirit out, which means this woman's body had been seized by this demonic spirit. This could have happened through an open door; the Holy Spirit didn't tell me why or how it happened, but it was there. We had to take authority over the demonic spirit for her healing to come. Yet there are other miracles that take something else. You need to know what the vehicle is for each miracle. How will it come to pass? What do you need to do in order to see it? Understand that there are different operations for different miracles.

Let's now look at the word *miracles* in the original Greek. If you have studied the New Testament or have been a believer for a while, then you'll probably recognize this word, *dunamis*.[4] We have used this word for many things, but it's the same Greek word that is used for *miracles*. You probably know *dunamis* as the Greek word for power. We use it for power all the time because of the famous Scripture early in Acts, where the Bible says that "you will receive power when the Holy Spirit comes upon you" (Acts 1:8 NLT). That's such a powerful phrase, and we've used it so many times. This verse is where we get the word *dunamis* from. The interesting thing is that the word used for *power* and *miracle* are the same word. So power is resting on you.

Many people have power, but they don't know they have it. Many people are carrying the power of the Holy Spirit in them. They've been filled, they pray in tongues, and they have the

Holy Spirit inside. But they don't even know what they really have sitting inside them. Going back to 1 Corinthians 12:10, where it says *the working of miracles*, again *working* means active, activate, operation, and we couple that with miracles, which is *dunamis*, meaning power. *Dunamis* doesn't just mean power, but by implication means a miracle itself, according to *Strong's Greek Lexicon*. It also means ability, abundance, might, strength, and a mighty or wonderful work.[5] When we couple these meanings together, the primary way we use *dunamis* is power, but Scripture says God has given to some the operation, or active power.

It's important to know that God calls this gift *active power* because you have the power of the Holy Spirit in you, but you're not going to see the fullness of that until you operate in it, or activate it. Some people have power in them, but the power isn't active; it's just sitting there. You have all this healing anointing and miracles locked up in you, but it's just sitting there in a potential state. It's sitting there in a dormant state, waiting to be activated. So when the Lord distributes this gift of *the working of miracles*, He's saying, *I'm giving you the gift to activate power!*

This power is in you, but you may not know how to use it. The gift of the working of miracles comes with divine instructions so that at the right time, when the situation comes up, you will know exactly what to do. You will know how to activate and operate in an ability that isn't yours. It's a supernatural ability from God that you cannot get from mankind. It comes with a gift when you need it the most—when a person is in a dire situation, when a person is at death's door, when the bank has told you no, you're not going to get the funding . . . Somehow the working of miracles stands up in you and the Lord gives you divine instructions about what to do, and you now know how to activate the power of God in you.

In Ephesians 3:20 the apostle Paul says, "Now to Him who is able to do exceedingly abundantly above all that we ask or think . . ." Paul goes on to say that it's "according to the power that works in us." In other words, it's according to how you work the power that's in you. It's according to how you're willing to activate it. If you want something bad enough, if you need to fast, you will turn your plate down for days, until you activate faith. If you want something bad enough, there are times that you just have to get the Word inside you, so all you do is listen to the Word and recite it until it gets in your spirit. Then when you encounter that situation, all that's coming out of your mouth is the Word, and you've been given the ability to activate power. As you are reading this, the Lord may be unlocking that gift and activating power in you right now. It's the ability to operate in the power that has been dormant inside you.

In order to operate, it's going to take faith.

In order to operate, it's going to take faith. The gift of the working of miracles is coupled with the gift of faith. The gift of faith is different from the fruit of faith. The fruit of faith in Galatians 5:22–23 refers to the attributes of God that should be evident in the life of the believer. The Spirit's fruits are necessary to support our foundational belief in Jesus Christ.

The gift of faith goes further than that, however. The gift of faith deals with a supernatural essence that comes upon you when your back is against the wall. You believe against all odds. It is believing God in the face of calamity, when things look as though the exact opposite of something good is going to happen.

You're going to need this kind of faith to operate in miracles. Faith is needed to unlock the miracles inside you. If you're a believer, the Lord wants to use you in the working of miracles.

MANTLE MOMENT

Pray this prayer as you finish this chapter about being mantled for miracles:

Father, I pray that You would open my eyes to see Your miraculous power working in and through my life. Your Word tells me in Romans 12:6 that spiritual gifts operate within us according to the measure of grace and faith that You give us. Lord, increase Your grace upon my life for miracles, and increase my faith to believe You for miracles. I pray for supernatural occurrences and encounters to manifest in my life and in the lives of those connected to me. Let the gift of miracles be activated and stirred up in my life, that I may bring glory to Your name. Let supernatural miracles be released as a sign and testimony to others about who You are. In Jesus' name, Amen!

9

THE LAW OF ACCUMULATION

If the clouds are full of rain, they empty themselves upon the
earth.

Ecclesiastes 11:3

In the mid-1920s, Henryk Grossman, an influential economics
professor at the free Polish University in Warsaw who turned into
a controversial communist revolutionary, came up with a theory
that later became known as the "law of accumulation."[1] Since
then, many entrepreneurs and leaders have adopted that law to
explain why tenacious efforts and even grassroots movements are
effective at making large-scale change globally. In an article about
how to apply the law of accumulation, entrepreneur and business writer William Ballard explained that this law simply says,
"A small thing accumulated over time can become a big thing."[2]

Often when I research specific laws and what the world has
adopted and used for success, it interests me to see that many
times, the roots of various popular principles come from the
Bible. The world has a way of taking spiritual principles and laws

and twisting them into what people want them to be. You see this with the "law of reciprocity," which states that people tend to feel obligated to return a favor. It can be further expressed as *if you do something kind, you will reap a kind reward.* Its biblical roots are found in Galatians 6:7, which tells us that "whatever a man sows, that he will also reap." People have learned that they can use this spiritual law while disregarding the things of God, but still reap financial blessings because they are generous. There are people in the world who are living off the benefits we have in the Church but aren't contributing. Biblical laws and principles are our birthrights, yet worldly sorts have tapped into them, twisted them, and used them illegally for their own benefit.

The world understands the law of accumulation, that a small thing accumulated over time can become a big thing. It's time now for the Church to understand that everything big had to start small. Everything big had to start somewhere. At times, we've gotten discouraged and frustrated because we've poured everything we have into a vision God has given us, but it doesn't seem as though the vision has grown. But in Zechariah 4:10 (NLT), the Bible tells us, "Do not despise these small beginnings, for the LORD rejoices to see the work begin." The New King James Version phrases it as "small things." It's interesting that in the Aramaic Bible in Plain English, the Aramaic translation records, "For who has despised the small days . . ." In fact, a number of translations make the word *days* plural there, not just one day. There are *days* of small beginnings. You may have to go through multiple seasons where things are small around you. Even though you know in your spirit that what you planted is big, nobody else can see it. You know that what the Lord has placed in you and the word He has given you will make an impact. At times, we've been looking for affirmation from other people, but they can't see that the seed God has placed inside us is big.

God told Jeremiah that he would build and plant. God put it that way because these functions are different sides of the same coin. People regularly say that God gave them something to build. This is not always physical; sometimes it's spiritual. Many people want to build, but they don't want to plant. Before you can build something, you must be willing to plant. You must get your hands dirty. You must be able to dig at the times when everyone else wants to rest. If we want to see a move of God in our cities, families, and churches, we must be willing to get our hands dirty. We must be willing to dig in the trenches until something happens. We cannot be ashamed and too prideful to humble ourselves and show God we'll do whatever it takes. We must be willing to serve until we see a move of God, even if nobody knows our name. If no one sees what we've invested, we must keep praying until we see the hand of God show up.

God is looking for people who can work at night, people not afraid to work when others are sleeping. Once you know what God has put in your spirit, the next step is to work. It's not time to draw back. We are not in a season where we can sit back and become lazy. This is the season to put our hands to the plow and push for the Kingdom. It's time for the Church to forcefully advance because God has opened an opportunity. There's a growing trend of people not wanting to work. Some who do want to work will only work if they can decide how they'll help and how they'll serve. There's a plentiful harvest, yet many don't want to be harvesters. We cannot become picky, because God is just looking for laborers, people who will say, "I'll do whatever it takes to see God move."

We are in a period where we are willing to work and to press. The Lord is calling you out of the cave. Some people have been in a place of burnout. Some have been saying, *Lord, I've got so much going on in my life . . .* But the Lord is saying, *I'm bringing you out of the cave of Adullam right now.*[3] *You were in distress, broken down, and you went in there for a reason. But you are not staying there. It's time to come out of that cave and get to work.*

We just saw that the Bible says, "Do not despise these small beginnings, for the LORD rejoices to see the work begin." This means that when you start a work inspired by God, heaven has a party. This means that God begins to rejoice because you started a Kingdom work. When God places something in your spirit that you're supposed to walk in, and it takes everything you have, and you have to sacrifice a lot, the Bible tells us that the Lord begins to rejoice. You may be reading this and may have just made the decision to start something in your heart. When you actually put your hands to the task, heaven is about to put on a celebration, because God is saying, *I'm rejoicing over you because you started.*

Don't underestimate the courage it takes to start something. We judge people who don't finish something, but we cannot underestimate the zeal and the boldness it takes for people to step out in faith and start something. If you've ever started a business, it takes courage to start. If you've started a family, it's going to take a whole lot of faith to sustain. When you step out to start anything it takes courage, and the Lord honors your willingness to start. He honors your obedience just to start it.

For instance, God may have put an early morning prayer time in your spirit, and the first morning may have been a struggle for you. You may have even been late. The Lord still honored your start. The accuser of the brethren will often come right after you start something to tell you how badly you're doing and what's not working. He will try to whisper in your ear what you're not doing right and bring up that you were late getting started. He will try to make you believe that you missed your time and try to make you lose sight of the fact that God honors and celebrates when we start. Even if you started late, just take time and thank God that you've started. Maybe you were supposed to do something twenty years ago. Just thank God that He allowed for another opportunity and that the season to start came back around.

Don't despise the days of small beginnings. When the Lord gave me an international ministry, He gave it to me in a store-front church with about twenty people. He said, *I'm sending you around the world.* I remember getting up in front of the people and saying, "By this time next year, we're going on our first international trip." They just looked at me and wondered how we would do that. I told them, "The Lord said we have to be there by this time next year."

When the Lord gives you specific instructions, you must learn how to obey Him. I learned early on not to worry about the provision portion of it because it's not my word. I didn't wake up and decide that I would just go to another country. And if I had done that, I wouldn't have gone to the country God specified. When you know that it's a word from the Lord, you can start rejoicing right there because when He gives you the word to do something or go somewhere, it means that He has already charted everything out for you. Everything has already been put together, and you just have to walk it out in order to see it come together.

It Starts with a Seed

I learned that God provides in the small things. He gives you a seed, but everything you need is in the seed. Even though everything you need is in that seed, you can still think you don't have enough. You think you're not courageous enough, or you think you're not educated enough, or maybe you think you don't have the qualifications. And maybe within yourself, you actually don't. But God said, *I gave you a seed.* In that seed from God might be a word in your spirit. Everything you need is in the seed.

Because that seed is so full, it takes time for it to develop. Something that helps the seed develop is rain. When the rain begins to come down into the soil, it waters the seed. Eventually, the seed begins to sprout. We talked about the law of accumulation. When the Bible says in Ecclesiastes 11:3, "If the clouds are full of rain, they empty themselves," it means there's a spiritual law that as things begin to build one on top of another, eventually there's going to be a downpour. As you keep putting the Word on that situation, as you keep speaking faith, you're just adding little by little. You think you're waiting on God, but you're not. He has set a spiritual law in place that when the clouds are full of rain, the rain is just going to come down. Water has been accumulating day after day. Your praise has been collected in heaven. There's a pot in heaven that has been filled with your praise. Even through sickness you kept on praising; even through pain you kept on worshiping. God said that little by little, you've been filling the pot. After a while, once it hits a tipping point, what you've been putting in that pot, what you've been sowing, is just going to spill over. You won't have to wait for God to then decide; He has already decided. And the more you sow into the pot, and the more you place praise and worship in there, the more you can rest assured that eventually, heaven is going to respond to you.

The outpour we're about to see will come because we've been fasting and praying, and we've been putting the Word on it. You've been declaring the Word of the Lord over your family for years, so this family revival you're about to see is coming from the years of rain accumulation. It's coming from the years that the water has been collecting. It's coming from years, and it hits a tipping point. You must believe that God is a God of His Word. If He said He would do it, it's just a matter of time. He's going to rain down on your family. He's going to rain down on your life. Rest assured that the clouds are about to empty themselves over your life.

The clouds are about to empty themselves in your church and mine, too. What we've been seeing manifest over the past couple of years within our ministries has been an accumulation of things over the past decade. People see the hand of the Lord on you when it's visible, but what they don't know is when God is moving behind the scenes. They don't know the prayer walks you have to do. They don't know the times you have to turn your plate down. They don't know the times you fasted and didn't broadcast it to anybody. They don't know the times you sacrificed in prayer until you had an encounter with Jesus Christ.

I have had people come to me who were trying to access the spiritual realm illegally, without Jesus. They've asked me what my secret was. They were compromised spiritually, but they read the Bible and went to church. What they couldn't understand, of course, is that our secret is in Jesus Christ! It's believing in the Lord our God. They didn't understand that it was day after day after day of water accumulating. It was week after week of not letting go of what God had said, even in the face of darkness. It was month after month when the devil said, *It's going to fail*, but God said, *It's not!* It was holding on to the promise of God. It was year after year, and eventually, when things hit a boiling point in the spiritual, the clouds just emptied out. When you accumulate enough water, it's not just going to rain for one day. It's not just going to rain for one hour. It's going to be raining for weeks in your life.

Get ready for the rainy season to break out over your life. You must believe that something has been building over time. You must know that all your prayers were not in vain. The prayers we've been praying over our cities and nations are not in vain. Even when you see violence in your city, God is about to show you a switch in the spirit where what the enemy meant for evil, God is about to turn it around for your good.

When the Lord began to show me the principles of this spiritual law of accumulation model, here are two things He said:

- *Don't despise the small thing. (You cannot despise the days of small beginnings.)*
- *You must be consistent.*

The Lord is giving you an assignment, so don't let go. The Bible says that you will reap if you don't faint (see Galatians 6:9). You are going to reap, and the enemy knows that he cannot take your harvest away from you. The only thing he can do is try to trick you out of it. He'll try to get you to let go before your time. There are so many people the enemy has been able to trick out of their place in God, sending them off in some other direction. That's what the assignment of the enemy is— to get into your thinking, to the point where you begin to say, *Well, maybe I won't do this. Maybe I'll go do something else instead.* The enemy comes to trick you out of your place. Don't let him! Remember that the rain is coming, and that the seed you've been planting is going to sprout into something a lot bigger than the seed itself.

Where the Blessing Meets You

Where does the blessing of the Lord meet you? The blessing meets you in your assigned place. When the Lord sent me to Minnesota, I told God, *It's cold there!* I just wanted to be sure that He really wanted me to go. But I knew what I had heard from the Lord. I really wanted to be in Hawaii or somewhere nice. I asked God if He would allow me to plant a church somewhere like that. What the enemy will try to do is trick you because he understands that what God is about to rain down must meet you in your assigned place.

We can't just do what we want. We can make a decision, but it's the Lord who has to have the final say-so in our direction and our path. There was a time when I was trying just to do it my way. I didn't want to do what God wanted me to do. I fought the Lord for two to three years because I didn't want to move to Minnesota. When I began to yield to the Spirit of the Lord, however, He began to put a love for Minnesota in my heart. Even though I was trying to go my way, what the Lord had for me was in the place He was sending me. That's where His blessing would meet me.

Where the blessing of the Lord meets you is always in a specific location because when the rain begins to come down and pour, it's not going to search for you in another place. It's not going to find you over in the place that you always dreamed of. It's going to find you right there where you were supposed to be the whole time.

Some people have moved out of their position too soon. Some have stepped out of their assignment. Praise God when we are found faithful in our assignment when the rain comes. We must be consistent, and we must be willing to press through the warfare. You must be willing to press through the trials, deal with demonic spirits and their agendas, and not break under the warfare and pressure. You have to be willing to face opposition and keep on moving. You have to be so consistent with this that you don't give up, even when it's easier. When it's easier for you to give up, it's a whole lot harder for you to keep your hand to the plow. It's a whole lot harder for you to keep on pushing. But there is a reward in the push, if you will just keep pushing. If you will keep pursuing what God says belongs to you, eventually the clouds are going to empty themselves. Eventually, it's going to come to pass.

Learn to Build Systematically

Whenever the Lord gives you instructions, take them in increments. You can't just rush into assignments. Some people are so zealous that when God gives them an assignment, they get excited about it on day one. But as the days carry on, the excitement diminishes, and the reality of the work and the cost starts to set in. When we don't take things in bite sizes, we begin to lose our zeal as we go along. The only way to prevent this is by learning how to work in stages. We have to learn how to be content with the phase and the stage we are in. Many times, we're trying to jump to level 10, but we have not done our work on level 1. Level 10 is coming, just hold on! But level 1 needs your attention right now. The day will come when the blessing of the Lord begins to overtake you in that area at the highest level, but right now what God needs you to do is the foundational work—the stuff people can't see.

One of my businesses is rehabilitating houses. What I learned early on rehabbing houses is that everybody wants to do the part where you're picking out the flooring and you're putting up the fixtures and you're choosing the nice paint. But if the foundation is not intact, and if the structure is not in order, you can try to paint over it all day long. You can try to put up a new light fixture and slap a coat of paint on it, but it's not going to work out for you. The house will look nice for a short while, but it won't have the longevity. What we must understand is how to break things down into stages. We want to jump levels, but the Lord wants us where He put us at this time. We must work our current stage, and trust that acceleration will hit our lives in due time. Have faith that you will make it to your next stage, but work on the stage and the level you are on right now. Take the time to develop the skills and learn the lessons. Make sure your foundation is intact.

The enemy tries to tempt you to look at somebody else who is seemingly at a more advanced place than you are. But if you begin to compare stages and covet what other people have, then you've fallen into the snare and trap of the enemy. You don't understand what stage others are on and what sacrifices it took for them to get to that place. But if you wait, there will come a season when you have the skill set God has been developing in you, and the anointing that rests on your life will be needed. Don't you dare change yourself to try to be someone else, because the world is not looking for another one of that person. The world is waiting on you to stand up and be who God has called you to be.

This is where you stand up in Christ's identity and be yourself. Some people are looking around and comparing themselves to other people. They start trying to compete, and sooner or later they will run out of energy, resources, and money. If we would just walk out our process, then the Lord would give us everything that He promised. All we need is in our seed from Him, not someone else's.

You can't compete with someone else's level. What you can do is compete with who you used to be. When you know where God brought you from, and when you know that you used to be depressed, when you know that you used to be addicted, when you know that you used to be a procrastinator, you will allow the Holy Spirit to work in you and make lasting changes. The Lord is growing you up. The Lord is saying it's time for you to grow. It's time for you to grow in character and in stature. We don't have time in the Body of Christ to compete with each other when He has Kingdom work for us to do.

What You Do Should Help Others

When dealing with the law of accumulation, it's not about just me and my unit. So many have that mindset, even within the Church. One of the reasons we have that mindset is because we've watched people make it out of hard situations and we begin to wonder when we will make it out. We've watched them growing in whatever area, and we start questioning God about when we will finally grow. That's a "crabs in a barrel" mentality to believe that if others make it, then it takes away from you. The Lord is killing that spirit in the Church because true unity knows that when you make it, I just made it.

I was once helping somebody who asked me how much money I was getting from it. This person asked what kickback

I got from helping, and assumed I was working with the company and being paid for it because I was really pushing hard for him or her. The person didn't understand why. I had to say, "I'm not making a dime. I actually don't get anything from helping you, other than the fact that I have this assignment from the Lord to help."

We have to be that kind of Christlike individual where we're willing to help our brothers and sisters and not look for anything in return. We have to be willing to help without looking for pay. We help because we're on assignment from heaven to help. We don't have to be acknowledged publicly. Our assignment from God is to help open a door that has been shut in someone's life. If the Lord has anointed us to help, then we have to be willing to break that door down, if that's what it takes.

I believe God is anointing you to help someone right now. If you see your brother or sister in Christ fall, you're going to pick that person up in the spirit. When you see people struggling, you're going to teach them what you have learned. You're going to teach them what the Holy Spirit has taught you. You're going to teach them what took you ten years to learn, and you're going to give it to them in two minutes. God is anointing some teachers and some door openers. You are one of them because you're willing to help someone else. God can trust you because you're willing to open a door. And because you're willing to help someone who is struggling, God is releasing resources. Take some time to pray over yourself where you are. Decree, "God is anointing me to help. He is giving me an anointing to help my family. He is giving me an anointing to help my community." I believe an anointing is coming on your head right now. This anointing will cause you to think differently because you're going to help someone else.

Jesus must be at the center. As I said at this chapter's start, people try to use these laws apart from God, but it won't benefit them in the long run. The Lord told me, *You've got to make sure that you're centered on Me, that you're Christ-centered in what you do.* It's easy to go help somebody and take a picture of yourself doing it. When Jesus is at the center, however, you can feed people and protect their dignity by not putting them on social media. Jesus taught us that whenever we gave people a drink of water and clothed them, we did it to Him. Too often, we don't see Jesus in people. It isn't about enabling people; it's about helping those who genuinely need the help and doing it unto Him.

Sometimes we make ourselves too busy to help others. One time I was on a ministry assignment, and I had to rush out to catch my next flight. I had to preach in another country, and I was about to miss the flight. I had just finished preaching and was headed to Africa next, and I was running through the hallway to get to my car. Along the way was somebody who had asked me to pray for him earlier in the day, and he was desperate. I had told him I would do it in the service, but the service took place, and the Lord didn't flow that way. After I turned the mic over, I was running to catch my flight. On my way, I saw this same man way back down the hallway. The Holy Spirit said to me, *Turn around and go back and fulfill that vow you made to him.*

I turned around, but my flesh was worried about missing the flight. I ran all the way back down this long hallway, but the man had already returned to the service. So I had one of the staff members go into the service and get him. I didn't know his name, and it was packed. They had to find him in the crowd, and they brought him out. I began to pray and prophesy over his life and his future. All the things God spoke came to pass within the next couple of years for him, and he became my host whenever I would return to his country. Oh, and after this wonderful ministry detour, I still made my flight!

What the Lord showed me through this scenario is that even though He is helping someone else through us, He is creating avenues for us. In the law of accumulation, it's about the many, it's about the collective, it's about everybody going up together, and it's about us growing together in Christ. That's what the Church is about, the *ecclesia*. It's about us growing together.

Keep Jesus at the Center

If we're going to say we are doing a Kingdom work, how can we do it without keeping Jesus at the center? Jesus' name should be larger than the one doing the work in His name.

It's dangerous to put an individual at the center of things. We must be careful not to accumulate the wrong things. If Jesus is not at the center, then something else has to be. It's easy to make profitability and personality the center. But Jude 1:11–12 says,

> Woe to them! For they have gone in the way of Cain, have run greedily in the error of Balaam for profit, and perished in the rebellion of Korah.
>
> These are spots in your love feasts, while they feast with you without fear, serving only themselves. They are clouds without water, carried about by the winds . . .

When the Bible refers to these people as "clouds without water," it means they have a form of godliness, but no power. There is no real anointing behind them. They are not accumulating water in order to pour it out. We will know people by their fruit. The foundation of everything has to be love. If love is not in it, it is not God.

Learn How to Be Disciplined

We must be willing to sacrifice what we want for what we need. Discipline is almost becoming a lost art, but that's why we are called *disciples*. We are students. We're supposed to be disciplined; we're supposed to be followers of Christ. We should be ever learning at the feet of Jesus.

One sign that you're struggling with discipline is the inability to keep your mouth closed. We must know how not to speak when it isn't time. Whenever people cannot seem to bridle their tongue, then they are usually feeding their flesh more than their spirit. Whatever is fed the most will take control and become the loudest in their life.

Many have confused their lack of discipline with demonic activity, and sometimes it's not a demon problem, but a flesh problem. Even after a person has undergone deliverance, there's another step that's called maintenance. The spiritual house must be furnished, and that takes discipline. That's the only way not to return to the sin you came out of. If the mind is not renewed, the enemy will always regain a foothold even if the demon has been cast out. And if your mind is not renewed, the enemy will have you thinking you're still bound. And so therefore as a man thinks in his heart, so is he (see Proverbs 23:7). Because you think you're bound, you are.

The apostle Paul told us to renew our minds continually (see Romans 12:2; Ephesians 4:23). The modern translation of that is, you've got to get saved every day. We've got to get into the presence of the Lord and go back to the altar every day. When we have discipline, we begin to renew our minds every day. You renew your mind by rehearsing the Word of the Lord. You know your mind isn't renewed if you haven't been studying your Bible. Declaring God's Word also helps renew your mind.

Your mind is the key to your directions and decisions. It's the key to everything you're about to enter into. Either you will see the power of accumulation work for you in the positive, or in the negative. The Bible says that "all things work together for good to those who love God, to those who are the called according to His purpose" (Romans 8:28). That Scripture actually works in the inverse if people are doing the opposite.

You will actually see all things work against those who are not called according to their purpose—meaning they are not in alignment with God's purpose for their lives and they are not operating in His love. You will literally see things within your world and life work against you until you get in alignment with the Word and will of God. Some people are declaring that all things work together, but instead what they're doing is living out an "all things work against" life. Discipline is the key to turning that around.

Fully Believe the Word of God

We must fully believe the Word of God, and everything we do that is for purpose and on purpose should be done for others. We are here to serve. We are here to help one another, and in turn, we reap what we sow.

For about three years, the Lord allowed Elijah to shut up the heavens so there would be no rain. Several things were going on when the heavens were shut up over that region and its people. The first thing was that the Lord had declared He was judging what was happening within that region, specifically what was happening in the house of Israel and what was going on concerning Ahab and Jezebel. He was judging it because the people turned from him and began to worship Baal. They began to worship idols and started mixing Baal worship with the worship of Yahweh. They didn't want to choose. In 1 Kings 18:21, Elijah asks them, "How long will you falter between two opinions? If the LORD is God, follow Him; but if Baal, follow him."

The same verse says that the people were completely silent. They didn't give a response. But when Elijah had shut up the heavens over that area for three and a half years, it was also a sign to these Baal worshipers. They believed that when there was a drought, it meant that their false god was angry with them. When there was no rain, they saw it as an omen that there was a curse over the people. So what the Lord had Elijah do was pronounce judgment in layers. In Old Testament times the people lived in an agricultural society, so when the Lord would bless His people, it was often manifested in agriculture. When the Lord was pleased with the people, they would have a great harvest and great crops. He told them, "If you are willing and obedient, you shall eat the good of the land" (Isaiah 1:19). But when the people would rebel and do wrong, then their crops would fail. There would be drought, and the earth would become very hard.

Blessing or judgment came in that way because they lived in an agricultural society. Often when God wanted to bless His people, when there was a great move of the Spirit or something the Lord wanted to do, He would begin to move on the agriculture. You would see the fruit of the land begin to grow, and the people would take in a great harvest. The earth would mirror what was happening in the heavens. And it wasn't just that way back then. It's also that way now. When something is going on that's disruptive in the earth, it's because there's something disruptive in the spiritual world. When we see the manifestations of it, whether in killings or any other kind of craziness going on, it's not coming out of nowhere. It means that over time, things have accumulated to that point.

We see the very same thing in the New Testament. What took place in Acts chapter 2 was the fulfillment of what was spoken in Joel chapter 2. God said, "And it shall come to pass in the last days that I will pour out of My Spirit on all flesh; your sons and your daughters shall prophesy, your young men shall see visions, your old men shall dream dreams" (Acts 2:17; cf. Joel 2:28). We quote that all the time, but we miss what happened a few verses before that in Joel. A few verses before this awesome promise, there was a famine, and a plague of locusts came and ate up all the crops. It was so bad that the locusts began to devour every single kind of crop there was, and the land was literally in a drought on top of that.

It's Getting Ready to Rain

Yet because of God's love and mercy, drought doesn't last forever. Going back to Elijah's story, we read in 1 Kings 18:1, "And it came to pass after many days that the word of the LORD came to Elijah, in the third year, saying, 'Go, present yourself to Ahab, and I will send rain on the earth.'" Elijah goes to present himself to the king, and in verse 41 he tells Ahab, "Go up, eat and drink; for there is the sound of abundance of rain." And the prophecy was fulfilled. The rain came in abundance.

In Joel 2, we find another instance in Scripture where the prophetic word came that a famine would end. The people were looking at not only a crop failure, but also a drought so that they couldn't grow anything. In the middle of that famine, here comes the word of the Lord saying, "And it shall come to pass afterward that I will pour out My Spirit on all flesh" (verse 28). But God didn't stop there. He also says, "I will restore to you the years that the swarming locust has eaten" (verse 25). The people lost years of crops in one day. In one day, they lost years of investment, so the Lord says, *I know you're in a famine right now, but I will restore the years that you lost.*

Now, that word came in Joel 2, but it wasn't fulfilled until Acts 2, where God says again that He will pour out His Spirit on all flesh. We understand that 120 people were waiting in the Upper Room in Acts. The reason they were gathered together at that time was because it was a holiday period, the Feast of Weeks. The Greeks began to call it Pentecost because it came fifty days after Passover, but the actual holiday period was the Feast of Weeks—the celebration of the grain harvest coming in. It was an agricultural Thanksgiving.

Jesus had told the disciples, *I want you to wait until I send My Spirit, and it's going to be poured out on you in a different way.* The Holy Spirit had already made His grand introduction in Genesis chapter 1, when He hovered over the face of the deep until something came up in the earth (see verse 2). Then there were many times throughout the Old Testament where the Holy Spirit was right there walking with men and women on the earth. But there was never a time until Jesus that the Holy Spirit lived inside an individual. Not just on a person, but in a person.

The reason God chose to send His Spirit fifty days after Passover was because that was at the same time as the agricultural harvest His people were celebrating. A Pentecost experience has everything to do with your harvest, and it has everything to do with what you are about to reap. The reason God chose to pour out His Spirit on the Feast of Weeks is because while His people were celebrating the grain harvest coming in in the natural, it was typifying the spiritual, where they were celebrating that the Holy Spirit was being poured out everywhere.

We are about to see the Holy Spirit move in a Pentecost anointing. He is about to be poured out once again on the people, and it's going to show up in your land. He's going to show up in your natural life, and you're going to see it with the fruit around you. Get ready to see it manifest on your job, and don't think it a strange thing. When the Holy Spirit starts pouring out around you and you start seeing God expand your house and your business and your ministry, don't think it a strange thing. He always pours out on a grain harvest when He gets ready to manifest Himself. He will dispel lack. He will move it out of your life and bring provision in the midst of it.

We're about to see the Lord do something so powerful, and He has already started. It's the Word spoken about in the Scripture that says, "I pray that you may prosper in all things and be in health, just as your soul prospers" (3 John 2). The work of the Holy Spirit is an inward work, an intrinsic work, a work people can't always see. People can't see when He's working on your character, when He's working on your heart, when you're being transformed to be more like Jesus. But after you reach a point of maturation, it begins to spill over into your life.

We're about to see an outpouring of the Holy Spirit. He's pouring into your spirit right now, but it's about to spill over into every other part of your life! You're not just going to be speaking in tongues. In the book of Acts, when the Spirit of God was poured out on the people, the next thing that began to happen was souls being added to the Church, meaning people got saved. God added souls by the thousands, and then the believers began to disciple them, and churches were set up in many places. Then they came together with all their resources and began to bring their money together.

I find that the government was okay with the early Church believers as long as they were just speaking in tongues. The government was okay as long as they were looking as if they were drunk in the streets. But the government got upset and put a curfew on them when they decided to have all things in common. The persecution started when the believers said, "We'll bring our property together, and we'll start bringing our resources together, and if we want to, we'll buy up the whole city."

The government got upset about that because the believers started to amass wealth. Not just natural resources, but lasting wealth. When the Lord gives you wealth, it's a spirit you carry. Having the spirit of wealth on you—which is good and not to be confused with the evil spirit of mammon behind the love of money—means that you appear prosperous on your poorest day. The spirit of wealth also carries the peace of God with it. The spirit of wealth doesn't always mirror the money that's in your actual bank account. If you're growing in money while you're growing in sin, that's not the blessing of God. God is putting the spirit of wealth on His people to prepare the Church for the coming famine. The way that we'll not only survive but thrive in the things that are coming is by accumulating what resources we have. The sign of the law of accumulation being at work will be that your personal economy is going up while the economy around you is declining. You will then be able to employ and sustain others.

When Elijah told Ahab to get up and eat and drink because it was getting ready to rain, the king did as Elijah said. Then Elijah went to the top of Mount Carmel and bowed his face to the ground. He heard the sound of rain, but nothing was coming yet (see 1 Kings 18:42). So he had to put himself in a position of intercession. Some moves of God can only be birthed out through prayer. Not only did he put his face to the ground, but he put his face between his knees. He was agonizing in intercession. As he was in intercession, he told his servant to go and look toward the sea and tell him what he saw. The servant returned and reported that he didn't see anything (see verse 43).

Elijah continued to prophesy even through what he didn't see. He sent his servant back six more times, and the servant continued to report not seeing anything. Elijah just kept praying. This was the law of accumulation in operation. It wasn't until the seventh time that the servant reported seeing something, but it was only a cloud the size of a man's hand (see verse 44). That doesn't make natural sense because there's no way a cloud the size of a man's hand can water a whole region that has been in a drought for three and a half years.

Except for the law of accumulation in the spiritual. That little cloud wasn't accumulating water; it was accumulating the word of the Lord. That little cloud began to expand to the point that the entire sky became dark. After a while, the heavens opened up. And when the rain came, acceleration came on Elijah. He ran so fast that he outran Ahab's chariot and beat him to the city (see verse 46). I prophesy over you and your family that the rain is coming. I prophesy that the rain is bringing increase, accumulation, and acceleration. Praise God for the rain!

MANTLE MOMENT

Whether you know it or not, the clouds are gathering water, and little by little there's a divine accumulation happening within your life. You don't have to see it in the natural; you don't have to feel it. Just know by faith that your clouds are filling up, and they will empty themselves. As a simple assignment, focus on the small dreams you have, the ones you wrote down in the "Mantle Moment" from chapter 1. Now begin to envision and write down the stages of growth that you see for those dreams growing and developing. And get ready for the rain.

10

MANTLED FOR THIS TIME

A man's heart plans his way, but the LORD directs his steps.

Proverbs 16:9

"Have a great day, and thank you for shopping with us" were the words that flowed out of my mouth so effortlessly. I was working at a dead-end job in a customer service position for a company in my city. I took care of purchases, scanned documents, faxed paperwork, and dealt with some customer complaints. When the company found out I had other computer skills, they created work for me to do that wasn't even in my job description, and they made me come up with the pricing for it. Yet I was barely earning above minimum wage at the time.

It was impossible to live off that small check, but by the grace of God, I managed. I informed my boss that weekends were difficult for me. I wasn't able to work on Sundays. He was highly upset and retaliated by cutting my hours drastically. What my boss and co-workers didn't know was that I was a minister and was part of the leadership team at my church. By this time, I had already been traveling and preaching in many different states and was an administrative pastor. But I had hit a point where I was tired of the process and all of the challenges that came with ministry. I loved God with all my heart and loved His people, but I passionately belted out to God in prayer, *I just want a normal life!*

At this point in my life, I had already experienced the trauma that comes with being *called*. I knew what it was to be rejected and hurt by those within the Church. My family and I had experienced so much warfare that I longed just to be like everyone else. My plan was to serve the Lord, but in a nice, quiet, *normal* way—getting married, having kids, and living in a nice house. My dream was to work in corporate America. I had always had a business mind, and I imagined the excitement of being challenged by climbing the ladder in a corporate setting. Yeah, sure, I was in a dead-end job now, but I had plans!

I made the decision that I wouldn't tell anyone on my job or anyone outside my very small church that I was a Christian. After all, I wanted a normal life, whatever that is. I just wanted to fit in. I focused on my goal and went to work. Day after day I would work, be friendly, and try my best to run in the opposite direction of my calling. Soon, however, a co-worker came up to me and started dumping her problems about her family and relationship on me. She was really going through some tough things. I thought to myself, *Why is she telling me this?* I listened to her and said a few small but polite words back, as any human being would.

The next day, another co-worker came to me and started dumping his problems on me. This happened repeatedly. Inwardly, I began to panic. I thought, *God, why are they coming to me?*

Pretty soon, a group of my co-workers came to me and said, "There's something different about you! We can tell. We feel so comfortable telling you our problems. It's like you know what to do. Who are you? What do you do outside this job?"

Inside, I was screaming, *This can't be happening!* It's as if God allowed these unbelievers to see me in the Spirit. They had never met me before working with me. They had never heard of me outside our workplace. Yet they knew something was different. Eventually, the doorway to minister to them opened, so I did. I felt as if God had blown my cover.

In spite of this series of events on my job, I was determined to be normal and put ministry behind me. One time I went to the movie theater, as I had done so many times before. I loved going to see the latest action, comedy, or sci-fi movie. This time, I went up to the ticket counter to get my ticket and the guy behind the counter says, "Sir, what church do you go to? I know you're a believer; I can see it on you. Are you in ministry?"

I said, "Really, is it that obvious?"

He replied, "I can see a light on you."

I realized at this point that the Lord was making it clear to me that I couldn't run. No matter where I go, He's there. No matter where I find myself, the calling of God still remains on my life. I quickly repented and gave up my dream of a "normal life" for His purpose instead.

Sometime after that, I was called to do some ministry in another state. I got the time cleared with my job, as I often did. When I got on the plane, my boss called me, literally shouting, "You better turn back around and *get yourself back here* to this job! I never give anybody this time off, *and there's no exception for you!*"

I explained that he had indeed given me the time off. He had approved it, and I had the proof. He continued screaming at me to get back to work immediately. I sat on the plane, confused, thinking, *Now that I've decided to obey God, things start going wrong.*

The Lord spoke to me that the time had come for me to take a leap of faith. I had to fulfill my ministerial mandate, while going into business for myself. When I heard this in my spirit, immediately my boss called me back as if he were a different person. He said in the calmest, most well-mannered voice, "Joshua, I apologize for the way I acted. Don't worry about anything. You go ahead and enjoy your trip. Everything's fine."

Confused at what had just happened, I went ahead with the ministry assignment and the Lord moved in a phenomenal way. Although I stayed on that job for a while afterward, I knew that God was allowing my environment to push me out. I left that job as the Lord commissioned me to go into full-time ministry and start my own business.

Leaving that job and stepping out into ministry and entrepreneurship was the biggest leap of my life up to that time. As soon as I did it, everything around me dried up. The clients that I had for my business dissipated. The ministry doors closed. I went from being fruitful to being in what seemed like a spiritual drought. I felt upset, and to be honest, in my immaturity I was secretly angry with God. I didn't want to understand how God could tell me to leave what I was familiar with and then allow me to suffer.

To make matters worse, I was berated by people close to me who looked at what I had done as a dumb decision. I was scolded, lectured, and talked about as being lethargic and unwilling to keep a stable occupation. I cried out to the Lord, feeling embarrassed, hurt, and as though somehow I had missed God. For six months, the Lord didn't speak to me about my situation. I thought I had failed Him in some way. I decided, *I'm going back into the traditional workforce to get my job back, or get a better one.*

I had interviewed with a company months before taking the leap of faith, and they had offered me a job. The pay was better, and the hours were great. This company had told me that whenever I was ready, I could contact them and they would hire me. I called them, and to my surprise they said they couldn't help me. I had a business degree and was putting in hundreds of résumés, and no one would hire me.

A prophet who had no idea what was going on in my life came to me and said, "The Lord called you for this time, and you can't go back to a regular job. You're being called into ministry, and you'll work for yourself."

I looked at this person as if I had no clue what he or she was talking about. I was in rebellion because things hadn't gone the way I wanted. A week or so later, this same prophet walked up to me in a service, still having no idea that I had taken a leap of faith to leave my occupation and go into ministry. The word came forth again: "God said, *What you're trying is not going to work. You can put in as many résumés as you want, but I've called you to go into ministry.*"

This time, I was even more irritated. I thought *Lord, I stepped out and now I have no provision. I tried it your way, but now I'm going back.* But I quickly put on my poker face in front of this prophet and acted as if I had no idea what that word meant. I've since repented, but I laugh looking back at this moment. I was still fixed in my disobedience. I put in hundreds more résumés and dozens more calls to jobs and employment agencies. No one had any clue what my plan was or how I was in this spiritually resistant place. I came to another service, and here comes this same prophet a third time. I tried my best to avoid the encounter, but it was a small church, so there was no way around it. The prophet uttered these words in passing: "The Lord says, *It doesn't matter what you try; you will not be able to work a 9–5 job. That is not your purpose. You must go into ministry. You're going to be traveling and ministering so much that you won't have time to do what you used to do. I will provide for you!*"

This time, I went home and paced the floor, muttered some words in prayer, and paced the floor some more. *God, what do You want from me? What do You want me to do?*

After I went through six months of silence and wandering in what seemed like a wilderness, God finally spoke to my heart. He shared with me how He had called me for this time. He said, *I shut down everything in your life. I put you in this place, that you might see the pride that's been hidden in you. I'm rooting it out! I'm dismantling self-reliance. You must depend on Me. And now I'm shooting you forth like an arrow. I'm relaunching your ministry. You are being released to travel. You will travel, and you will minister abroad. You will do all that I send you to do.*

I was shaking, weeping, and crying in the presence of the Lord. This was truly an encounter. I repented to God of my immaturity, rebellion, and pride. My heart melted before Him, and in that moment I released all my resistance. It didn't matter where the money would come from; I was sure He would provide. It didn't matter what others thought; I had received a word from God that I was called for this time and that He had need of me for His Kingdom.

You Were Born for This Time!

If you're from my country, there's a reason why you weren't placed here in 1776. As much as the new world was forming and the contentious birth of America was at hand, you were simply a thought in the mind of God. You were with Him in eternity, but not manifested in the earth realm. You weren't placed here on this earth two hundred years ago, because you were born for the time when you were needed the most. When God fashioned you out of eternity into now, you were brought here on purpose and for purpose. The same is true for anyone. Whatever country you're from, your unique ability, God-given gifts, talents, and skills were needed at this exact point in history. The anointing on your life was given for *now*.

This is the reason why you shouldn't put off the calling of God or delay your obedience to the Father. Your calling is like an invitation to join in partnership with what the Holy Spirit is doing in eternity that's affecting the earth. God releases callings to people. Or in this analogy, He sends invitations out to those whom He selects. It's up to us to answer the call and walk in this supernatural partnership with Him. In Luke 14:16–24 (NIV), Jesus gives the Parable of the Great Banquet:

> A certain man was preparing a great banquet and invited many guests. At the time of the banquet he sent his servant to tell those who had been invited, "Come, for everything is now ready."
>
> But they all alike began to make excuses. The first said, "I have just bought a field, and I must go and see it. Please excuse me."
>
> Another said, "I have just bought five yoke of oxen, and I'm on my way to try them out. Please excuse me."
>
> Still another said, "I just got married, so I can't come."
>
> The servant came back and reported this to his master. Then the owner of the house became angry and ordered his servant, "Go out quickly into the streets and alleys of the town and bring in the poor, the crippled, the blind and the lame."
>
> "Sir," the servant said, "what you ordered has been done, but there is still room."
>
> Then the master told his servant, "Go out to the roads and country lanes and compel them to come in, so that my house will be full. I tell you, not one of those who were invited will get a taste of my banquet."

The invitations went out, but people were too busy. This parable is a prophetic representation of what some people today are doing when God calls them for a Kingdom assignment. Each person in the story is symbolic of the modern-day excuses we use. We must be aware of these excuses so that they don't become stumbling blocks to our purpose in God. Here's an interpretation of each excuse in the parable:

1. *I just bought a field.* This was the excuse of the first individual invited to the banquet feast. A field can be symbolic of your sphere of influence or the area you're called to work or serve in. It could be your career field, your field of study, your platform, or your ministry field. Sometimes when God's calling is on you, it can be an interruption to your field of interest. You must be willing to leave your field and pursue the heart and purpose of God for your life. In most cases someone accessing, or in this case buying, a new field would be a great thing. But when your field takes precedence over God, that's when it becomes a problem. Don't be so married to a career, interest, venture, or even a particular ministry that you can't come to the banquet table when God is calling for you to feast.

2. *I just bought five pairs of oxen.* This represents a lucrative business, or money. In Jesus' time, owning five pairs of oxen would have been a sign of a wealthy business. Some people refuse to answer the calling of God and take a leap into purpose, because they are blinded by money. Money has become the deciding factor for many. However, money is not more valuable than obedience to God. Money can't bring fulfillment. Money can't fill the voids and broken areas within your soul. Money is just a bartering/trading tool used within our society— nothing more! We must strip the idolatrous power that the world has given to money. It caused this man in Luke 14 to miss having a seat at the banquet table.

3. *I just got married.* The last individual said he couldn't answer the invitation to the banquet because he had

just gotten married. This is symbolic of using relationships and commitments as an excuse not to follow after God's plan for your life. Although marriage, covenants, and relationships are important, they should be properly prioritized within the scope of your calling and purpose. It's highly possible to have great, healthy, thriving relationships and still answer the calling of God on your life. You don't have to substitute one for the other. However, all the things we have, whether relationships, goals, or anything else, should be submitted fully under God. God should be first in everything.

In this parable, Jesus exclaims that the master of the house was angry that all of those who had received invitations had rejected them. He then told the servant to go into the streets and highways and bring in the lame, crippled, blind, and those of low social status. He called for those who didn't have a lot of money, and they all filled the banquet. This picture shows that many people will reject their calling, but God is looking for those who are poor in spirit, broken, challenged, or limited in some capacity to sit at His table. You don't have to have it all together. You don't have to be qualified. None of us are. Matthew 22:14 says, "Many are called, but few are chosen." This means that many receive the invitation to come to the banquet or be part of what God is doing, but few answer that call. The chosen are the ones who answer the call. That's why you are chosen, because God handpicked you and you are answering the call.

The Tipping Point

Right now, the world as we know it is at an inflection point. We have approached a tipping point in the Spirit. The crises, problems, and chaos in our world are a signal that it's time for you to rise. You can no longer hide; the Kingdom of God has need of you. You can no longer be silent; your voice is valuable. You can no longer sit back and just watch God use someone else, when He desires greatly to use you also.

You are being mantled for this time. This means God is equipping you with everything you need to face the challenges that come with your purpose, and you will be victorious. Every great leader in the Bible emerged at the point where there was a crisis. The gifts, calling, and anointing on David emerged at the time when Israel needed him the most. The greatness in David surfaced when the Israelite army was faced with a massive Goliath. Crisis brought purpose out of David and caused him to rise.

Esther emerged at the point when Israel needed her the most. She was strategically placed in a royal position so that at the right time, she could intercede on behalf of her people. Her uncle, Mordecai, informed her in Esther 4:14 (ESV), "For if you keep silent at this time, relief and deliverance will rise for the Jews from another place, but you and your father's house will perish. And who knows whether you have not come to the kingdom for such a time as this?" He let Esther decide if this was her moment. She had to be willing to meet the challenge ahead of her, standing firmly in the boldness of God.

Just like Esther, you must decide if this is your moment. Have you come to the Kingdom for such a time as this? I could answer yes for you, but it wouldn't really help you. You have to know within yourself, *I have been called to the Kingdom for this time!*

MANTLE MOMENT

You must realize that you have been mantled for this time. Nothing and no one can hold you back from walking in the fullness of who you are, except you. Take the next few minutes and think about any excuses you've allowed to enter your mind, which could be hindering your progression. What are these excuses? What was the door that allowed them to come in (whether fear, failure, trauma, etc.)? How do you plan to uproot these excuses so that you take up the mantle and move forward unhindered into God's purpose for you?

11

PASSING THE BATON

And His mercy is on those who fear Him from generation to
generation.

Luke 1:50

In middle school I ran track because I had no other choice; it
was part of our athletics requirement. I can still feel the rhythm
of my breathing—*inhale through your nose, exhale through
your mouth*. I can still feel the impact of my feet hitting the
combination of asphalt, rubber, and sand on the smooth surface of the track. I never intended to be a runner, but I found
out that I was good at it. I was the second-fastest person on the
entire campus when it came to sprinting and running a mile.

The long-distance races were where the stamina was needed.
I had to learn to start strong right away and pace myself in the
middle segment. Then power through at the end. According to
my coach I was extremely good, so they would send me along
with a select few to compete at statewide competitions. The relay
races were particularly interesting to me. It's an event where four

athletes run an equal distance broken up into segments. Once individual runners complete their sprint, they pass a rodlike object called a baton to the next person to continue the race. You had to function as a well-organized unit, a cohesive team.

When the baton is being passed, the next runner has to start running before the previous runner actually approaches. As the hand-off occurs, there's a short point where both the previous runner and the next runner are holding the baton together before it is fully passed. This is a prophetic analogy of what is happening now in every sector of the world. We are in an era shift, and there is a passing of the baton from one generation to the next and from one leader to the next. We are in the midst of a shift change. Those who have occupied seats of power and influence so they could effect change in our world will hand off their seats to a new regime.

A New Kind of Believer

Throughout New Testament Scripture, in the synoptic gospels Jesus addresses His earthly generation and the one to come after it. In Mark 8:12, He questions His generation's faith. They were constantly seeking for proof of anything that God revealed through Him, when the proof was right there in front of them: "But He sighed deeply in His spirit, and said, 'Why does this generation seek a sign? Assuredly, I say to you, no sign shall be given to this generation.'"

The word *generation* there is the Greek word *genea*.[1] It means an age or period of time, or a nation. When Jesus addressed a generation, as He often did, He wasn't speaking to a particular age group, as we use the word today. He was referring to a group of people. He was referring to a nation of people and an era or period of time.

Further, the Greek root word for generation is *genos*, meaning a kind, referring to species.[2] When God institutes a passing of the baton from one generation to the next, He is referring to the rising of a new group of people, a different kind of believer. Some call it a new breed. We will see the rising of the new thing that the Lord is doing. The passing of the baton will be accompanied by new models, new systems, new ways of doing things. The old way of doing things will quickly fade, as the . new thing is ushered in very quickly.

You are the new kind of believer whom the Lord is raising up. The baton is being passed into your hands to run this race, and you must run it well. As 1 Peter 2:9 says, "You are a chosen generation, a royal priesthood, a holy nation, His own special people, that you may proclaim the praises of Him who called you out of darkness into His marvelous light." Three main keys in this Scripture will help you understand why you cannot sit idly by. Rather, you must get in position and pick up the baton because *you are a chosen generation, you are a royal priesthood,* and *you are a holy nation.* Let's look at each of these keys.

You are a chosen generation.

God has chosen you to be part of the generation that must carry a unique assignment to the world. You have been chosen. The word *chosen,* in the original language 1 Peter 2:9 was written in, means favorite, select, and elect.[3] God's massive favor is on your life. You have been selected and elected to fulfill His purpose for your life in the earth.

You're not chosen because you are so skilled or talented. You've been chosen because the Most High has placed favor on you. Favor is a driving force that overshadows you with grace, mercy, and a supernatural endowment that empowers you to accomplish what He has for you to do.

You are a royal priesthood.

This means that you walk in a priestly anointing. You are called to minister and serve others as unto the Lord. In the Old

Testament, priests were the advocates on behalf of the people to God. They would make sacrifices for the sins of the masses. It was their responsibility to carry out sacred ministerial tasks in the holy of holies. They were a lifeline between God and His people. They represented more than just themselves. Now, because Jesus Christ fulfilled the law, priests no longer have to sacrifice rams and bullocks. People no longer have to talk to a priest in order to talk to God.

However, the priesthood is still important. Revelation 5:10 (NIV) says, "You have made them to be a kingdom and priests to serve our God, and they will reign on the earth." I've heard it said that the original Hebrew interpretation is "a kingdom of priests." The priestly role is still sacred and needed today. Priests are still intercessors called to serve others through the Word of God. You carry a priestly anointing, but you are also royalty. You are a son or daughter of the Most High God. Power and authority have been placed in your hands as Christ's representative in the earth.

You are a holy nation.

You have been set apart. Because you have been selected to carry the baton and lead in this new era, you can't be like everyone else. To be holy is to be called out from among the rest. It is to be set apart for a specific assignment.

Holiness is the standard for believers. We are to emulate the character of Christ. We are to flee from sin and pursue righteousness. It doesn't mean that we are perfect. None of us are perfect. But it does mean that we are after God's heart.

Finding Your Place in the Kingdom

Matthew 6:33 (KJV) instructs us, "But seek ye first the kingdom of God, and his righteousness; and all these things shall be added unto you." The Kingdom of God is not a physical place or structure; it's what I call a spiritual God-domain. Wherever the King reigns, you will find His Kingdom. If God reigns in your life, then you possess the Kingdom.

Many people live their lives feeling as though there's something missing. Some search for the missing pieces in people, places, or things, only to realize that they are still unsatisfied. You will live your life unsatisfied and unfulfilled until you seek and find your place in the Kingdom. Deep within you, God has placed a treasure hidden from human eyes. The apostle Paul declares, "But we have this treasure in earthen vessels" (2 Corinthians 4:7).

The Greek word *treasure* here is *thesauros*, meaning the place in which good and precious things are collected and laid up.[4] This place of collected treasures is the Kingdom of God, for Matthew 13:44 says, "Again, the kingdom of heaven is like treasure hidden in a field, which a man found and hid; and for joy over it he goes and sells all that he has and buys that field." It is clear that the Kingdom of God is a place of treasures, and it is hidden in you. Throughout history, you see that over time treasures and precious goods become lost or buried in the earth. In order to be discovered, they have to be dug out. This is a spiritual allegory. You have a place of treasure within you, but all the dirt has to be dug out of your life in order to find it.

Luke 17:21 (KJV) speaks this revelation: "Behold, the kingdom of God is within you." This Scripture reinforces the fact that there's a precious commodity in you called the Kingdom. Matthew 6:33 gives the command to seek first the Kingdom of God. Isn't it interesting that God told you to seek a Kingdom that's already inside you? Your journey in life will be uncovering this wonderful treasure He has placed within you. As I mentioned, in order to fully access it, you must dig out all the dirt covering it. Dirt represents anything unclean and ungodly. By allowing acts of sin, disobedience, and transgression against God, you block your access to the Kingdom.

As a believer, you must deny your flesh and make sure no works of the flesh are in operation. The seventeen enemies of the flesh written about in Galatians 5:19–21 are dangerous weapons against you and your possession of the Kingdom. Verse 21 says that "those who practice such things will not inherit the kingdom of God." If you have engaged in any of these works of the flesh, then there is need for repentance and cleansing in order to reclaim your possession of the Kingdom. The first step in finding your place in the Kingdom is removing any works of the flesh and reclaiming your inheritance. This inheritance was already promised to you. However, you must meet the necessary requirements in order to access it.

Four different references in the Bible reiterate that the unrighteous will not "inherit the kingdom" (see 1 Corinthians 6:9, 10; 15:50; Galatians 5:21). The word *inherit* in these references is the Greek word *kleronomeo*.[5] It means to "obtain by right." The righteous have a *right* to access the Kingdom. The word also means "to receive the portion assigned to one." Every believer has been allotted a portion of the Kingdom. You cannot find your place in the Kingdom unless you know your portion of the Kingdom. Everyone has a sphere, field, or area of interest that they are called to. As we continue to witness the passing of the baton, your sphere of influence will become highlighted. You will see clearly where you have been called to serve.

Understanding Your Measure of Rule

Ephesians 4:7 states, "But to each one of us grace was given according to the measure of Christ's gift." God distributes to everyone a measure of the gift of Christ. Christ was sent to restore to us that which Adam lost through disobedience to God (sin). The gift of Christ within us restores righteous rule and dominion. Christ gives us delegated authority to have dominion. Dominion is the right to rule over your assigned portion.

This is known as the "measure of rule." The word *measure* in Ephesians 4:7 is the Greek word *metron*.[6] It is the extent of your rule and standard of judgment determined by God. It is the portion that God has allotted to you. As aforementioned, I call it your God-domain.

The apostle Paul's ministry was used of God largely to impact the Gentiles. Acts chapters 20 and 21 span Paul's apostolic voyage from Ephesus to Caesarea, and then on to Jerusalem. In these chapters, you see that he had a measure of grace (*metron*) to reach the Gentile nations and to preach the Gospel. God used Paul to establish churches in these Gentile nations, and Paul saw a great harvest of souls. Although he faced opposition and was oftentimes challenged, he endured, and God delivered him out of all his troubles.

Paul's *metron* was largely seen in the Gentile nations. However, he had a strong desire to reach the Jews. In some instances, this took him beyond his measure of rule (*metron*). Acts 20:16 says, "For Paul had decided to sail past Ephesus, so that he would not have to spend time in Asia; for he was hurrying to be at Jerusalem, if possible, on the Day of Pentecost." It's clear that it was in Paul's heart to be in Jerusalem on the Day of Pentecost. Scripture reveals that it was Paul's decision to sail past Ephesus. Pay close attention to that. It shows that the Holy Spirit didn't tell Paul to do this; it was simply in his heart to do it.

The Holy Spirit will allow us to make decisions with the intelligent design we were constructed with, called our mind. Only when we veer from Him and His plan will He give us warning to change course. Look at Acts 21:4: "And finding disciples, we stayed there seven days. They told Paul through the Spirit not to go up to Jerusalem." Here is an interesting point, where the fellow disciples warned Paul by the Holy Spirit *not* to go up to Jerusalem. God was trying to keep Paul out of unnecessary danger.

Stepping outside your *metron* poses unnecessary danger. The great apostle was being persistent and wouldn't hear the Holy Spirit, even though he knew it was the Spirit of God speaking, telling him not to go. Paul had a passion beyond his measure of rule. You must understand that having a passion to do something just isn't enough if the Holy Spirit isn't backing it.

In Acts 21:10–11, the Lord used a prophet named Agabus to release a word of warning to Paul:

> And as we stayed many days, a certain prophet named Agabus came down from Judea. When he had come to us, he took Paul's belt, bound his own hands and feet, and said, "Thus says the Holy Spirit, 'So shall the Jews at Jerusalem bind the man who owns this belt, and deliver him into the hands of the Gentiles.'"

Not much is known of Agabus, whose name means grasshopper. Although he could have been viewed as an insignificant minor prophet, he had a word that could have saved the apostle Paul a whole lot of trouble. However, Paul continued to press beyond his *metron* out of zeal and a passion to minister to the Jews:

> Now when we heard these things, both we and those from that place pleaded with him not to go up to Jerusalem. Then Paul answered, "What do you mean by weeping and breaking my heart? For I am ready not only to be bound, but also to die at Jerusalem for the name of the Lord Jesus."
>
> So when he would not be persuaded, we ceased, saying, "The will of the Lord be done."
>
> Acts 21:12–14

Paul continued on with his journey, against the warning of the Holy Spirit. He went to Jerusalem anyway. Sure enough, he was bound, just as the prophetic word from Agabus had proclaimed. Although the apostle Paul had great impact with his ministry, he spent the rest of his life bound and imprisoned because he didn't hear when God told him not to go.

With each God-domain or *metron*, God assigns *delegated authority*. God grants you the right within your territory to give orders, make decisions, and enforce the laws. Delegated authority gives you the right to stand in God's stead. Therefore, when the inhabitants of your territory look at you, they see God in you! Everyone has a *metron* or portion of territory, even if it's just your home. In your home, you're the one who sets the rules and enforces the laws. Others have delegated authority that expands to their positions or their jobs.

Also, with your God-domain or *metron* comes *divine influence*. Influence is the capacity to have an effect on the character, development, and behavior of a person or group of people.[7] It is the power to persuade or lead people in a direction. Influence is not a bad thing when used inside proper spiritual guidelines. In order to be a leader in your domain, you have to have influence. With an anointing comes influence. Jesus had such influence that all He did was walk up to the disciples and say two words: "Follow Me." And they did follow because of the power of influence He had. If you're a prophet, God has to grant you with some measure of influence in order for people to listen to you or believe what you say. Second Chronicles 20:20 says, "Believe his prophets, and you shall prosper." That word *prosper* is the Hebrew word *tsalach*, which means "to advance, prosper, make progress, succeed, be profitable."[8] These are the benefits of following the *true* prophetic voice under the guidance of the Holy Spirit.

Staying within Your Measure of Rule

How important is it to stay within your measure of rule? Second Corinthians 10:12–15 stresses the importance of staying within your measure of rule and authority. When you compare yourself to others, you immediately enter the danger zone of going beyond your measure of rule, and you leave yourself wide open for insecurity:

> For we dare not class ourselves or compare ourselves with those who commend themselves. But they, measuring themselves by themselves, and comparing themselves among themselves, are not wise. We, however, will not boast beyond measure, but within the limits of the sphere which God appointed us—a sphere which especially includes you. For we are not overextending ourselves (as though our authority did not extend to you), for it was to you that we came with the gospel of Christ; not boasting of things beyond measure, that is, in other men's labors, but having hope, that as your faith is increased, we shall be greatly enlarged by you in our sphere . . .

Now, God can stretch you beyond your comfort zone or familiar place. However, we are not to stretch ourselves beyond our measure. To stretch beyond measure means that you extend beyond the territory God has given you. When it comes to ministry, everyone with a ministry has a certain portion, accompanied by certain physical territory. For instance, your ministry is given a specific territory. Even though as ministers we may often say that we desire to reach everyone, the fact of the matter is that we're each given a portion of people to reach. When we go outside that scope against God's will, we open ourselves up for unnecessary hardships. And God doesn't cover that which we do outside His will. The danger of going outside your *metron* is that you're left uncovered. The will of God is a covering for your life. His will is your protection, and in His will is your provision: ". . . and with the measure you use, it will be measured back to you" (Matthew 7:2).

It's clear that we are all given a measure and we are also measured to make sure we meet the standard of God for our lives. The word of Jesus Christ in Matthew 7:2 reveals that if you don't meet the measure, you don't access the domain God has for you. You've been given a *metron*, or a portion, but you must also meet the requirements for the measure given to you. When you don't meet God's measure or standard for your life, you place yourself in a position to lose the territory God has given to you.

MANTLE MOMENT

In this new era, mantles are passing, and the baton is changing hands. You must position yourself to grab the baton and run your race. In part, this comes by knowing your place in the Kingdom of God. Take a moment to pray and ask God to help you discover, or even rediscover, your field and sphere of operation in the Kingdom. Knowing this will help you carry the anointing God has given you with effectiveness and precision.

12

MANTLED FOR A MOVEMENT

But you will receive power when the Holy Spirit comes upon you. And you will be my witnesses, telling people about me everywhere—in Jerusalem, throughout Judea, in Samaria, and to the ends of the earth.

Acts 1:8 NLT

The next move of God will be greater than all the past movements combined. I believe that God is gracing His people for something greater than what we have ever seen. However, in order to understand where we're going, let's look back at an explosive movement that influenced the Church, society, and world. Several major movements throughout the history of America and the world have helped shape my country and also other nations into what they are today. Each movement has contributed to the development and progression of societies and nations.

Because I am so familiar with it, I want to talk specifically about a movement that has most impacted the United States.

As I do this, if you live elsewhere you can think about and compare movements that have impacted your own country. Here at home, no movement has been more revolutionary within the American Church than the Pentecostal movement of the early twentieth century. According to *Britannica*, Pentecostalism is a charismatic religious movement that birthed a number of Protestant churches in the United States. It is set apart from other religious movements because of its focus that all Christians should seek a post-conversion religious experience known as the baptism of the Holy Spirit.[1]

The term *Pentecostal* is derived from Pentecost. It refers to the experience in Acts 2 when the Holy Spirit was given to the early Church as 120 followers of Christ waited in the Upper Room. After fifty days of waiting, the Holy Spirit sat on each of them like cloven tongues of fire. All who were waiting were filled with the Spirit and began to speak in tongues. It was a radical phenomenon, and other people who witnessed it received salvation that same day. Many were added to the Church.

In the early twentieth century, the Pentecostal movement was groundbreaking. Not only did it cause new Protestant churches to arise, but it also affected societal norms, advanced the civil rights movement, and helped shape America's destiny. A few years back, I did some research for a seminary class on this movement and found out just how widespread its effect has been in all these areas. Because I think this is valuable for us all to realize, I want to include some of that research in the next two sections of this chapter. You may find them a bit more scholarly in tone, but I think you'll also find them very interesting and informative.

Pentecostalism's Historical Context

Pentecostalism is one of the most impactful developments in the recent history of Christianity. From America, it became a dynamic force around the world. Some credit Charles Parham, a preacher and evangelist in the late 1800s, with this. We'll talk more about him in a moment, but he started a ministry school where he was said to be the first to associate glossolalia (speaking in other tongues) with being filled with the Spirit.[2] He had a student by the name of Agnes Ozman. She was the first documented to be filled with the Holy Spirit and speak in other tongues in their time period. In the year 1900, there were only a handful of people who were experiencing what is known as the baptism of the Holy Spirit.[3] Charles Parham paved the way for Pentecostalism.

Most notably, however, the beginning of Pentecostalism can be traced back to 1906 at the Apostolic Faith Gospel Mission on Azusa Street in Los Angeles, California. It all started when an African American pastor by the name of William J. Seymour arrived in Los Angeles from Houston, where he had been learning at Charles Parham's ministry school. He had been invited to become the pastor of a small storefront Holiness church. He taught on the experience of those who had waited in Jerusalem in Acts 1:4–8 and Acts 2:4. He preached that this was the pattern the Church should follow. Believers should ask for the Holy Spirit, and then they could be baptized in the Spirit.[4] They would then have the ability to speak in other tongues. When Pastor Seymour initially started teaching this unconventional message, many of the members of his congregation didn't receive it. The denomination questioned his theology and fired him.

Thankfully, a couple attending the church allowed Seymour to stay with them. Seymour began sharing his teachings on the Holy Spirit as the couple invited people to hear him. The meetings outgrew their home, and then moved to another house. Many people got filled with the Spirit spontaneously. News of this outpouring spread to many of the area Holiness churches. Pretty soon, these believers were able to find a building. The building was in very bad shape, but they worked hard to fix it up. "By Easter Sunday, April 15, [1906] they had held their first meeting. It would soon be known the world over as the Azusa Street Mission."[5] The very next day, the *Los Angeles Daily Times* reported on this service. On the same day as the headline, there was a major earthquake in San Francisco and other areas of California. Many of the residents took this as a sign that God was working through the Azusa Street Mission. It was seen as some sort of an apocalyptic warning, calling people to repentance.

The Azusa Street revival grew very rapidly. Other churches questioned the validity of what was taking place. Notable pastors supported it, however. It snowballed into a citywide, and of course nationwide, eruption. The goal of the revival was repentance, increased prayer, evangelism, and especially the baptism of the Holy Spirit.[6] People from all walks of life gathered in this revival. They included immigrants, former slaves, and people of all races. The movement countered segregation and racism, which were societal norms at the time. In fact, Frank Bartleman (a reporter) would later observe that at the Azusa Street Mission, "the 'color line' was washed away in the blood."[7]

Although the revival sparked a flame throughout the country and even overseas, conflicts arose with the revival. Initially, pastors didn't embrace what was happening at the newly founded church on Azusa Street. As the revival continued, some questioned if the movement of Pentecostalism would last, or if it would just become another denomination or quickly fizzle out.[8] Of course, we know that it did not. While the revival was booming, another situation was occurring in Los Angeles. In his comparison between the Azusa Street Mission and historic black churches, author and church history professor Cecil Robeck commented, "Discrimination could be found mostly at more basic levels in Los Angeles. In August 1906, for instance several restaurants and hotels refused to provide services to

African Americans. Over the next nine months, others would join them, making it clear that African American trade would not be welcomed."[9] African Americans were at the helm of the origins of Pentecostalism, but were also being grossly mistreated. Although the revival stated that there were no lines of color, those just could not be avoided. Some believe that this is the reason the Azusa Street revival came to an abrupt end.[10] Yet while the birthplace of Pentecostalism may have disseminated, clearly the movement never died.

The Pentecostal Movement's Leadership

The Pentecostal movement had two major figures. The first, Charles Parham, can be seen somewhat as the father of Pentecostalism. Parham was the founder of the Apostolic Faith Movement. He had been brought up in Holiness and Methodist churches. He became a prominent preacher and evangelist. He began instructing students in a school of ministry that he conducted in Kansas and Texas. At the turn of the twentieth century, he was teaching his students that they needed to be baptized in the Holy Spirit and fire. He taught that this should be expected of all those who converted to Christianity.[11] He proclaimed a message of holiness and sanctification.

Parham was marked for greatness as a young child. In his own words, he says, "The earliest recollection I have of a call to the ministry was when about nine years of age, and though unconverted, I realized as certainly as did Samuel that God had laid His hand on me, and for many years endured the feeling of Paul, 'Woe is me, if I preach not the gospel.'"[12] He spent his life doing the work of ministry and pioneering in Christian movements. He is significant to the Pentecostal movement because he lit the match that started it all. He had the first documented cases of people being filled with the Spirit and speaking in other tongues in that time period. In addition, he taught William J.

Seymour about the baptism of the Holy Spirit, prayer, revival, and the gifts of the Spirit.

William J. Seymour is the second major figure in the Pentecostal movement. As I mentioned earlier, he started the Azusa Street revival, the birthplace and epicenter of the movement. This took Pentecostalism throughout America and beyond. The information on Seymour's life is spotty due to the time period and the fact that he was African American. Not many records were kept for African Americans because they weren't treated as equals. The *Encyclopedia of American Religious History* does provide some information for us.[13] He was born in Centerville, Louisiana, on May 2, 1870, as the son of freed slaves. He received no formal education, and he worked as a waiter in Indianapolis for a time. In 1900 Seymour moved to Ohio, where he encountered and became part of the Holiness movement. He had an experience of sanctification there. These encounters in his formative salvation years were preparing him to be a catalyst in the Pentecostal movement. Later, Seymour settled in Houston, Texas, where he met Charles Parham and attended his Bible Institute.

These two men are integral to the Pentecostal movement because they sacrificed their lives carrying out the Gospel mission. They served the people whom they were assigned to minister to. They trained up disciples, and more importantly, they taught the importance of the baptism of the Holy Spirit. This was all done during a time period where not many in the Western world were filled with the Spirit. Seymour and Parham also ushered in the movement of the gifts of the Spirit. People began to have supernatural, spontaneous encounters with God. These men taught that every believer should seek a Holy Spirit baptism after salvation. This was new and not the current doctrine.

These two men were met with enormous challenges. In particular, Seymour was an African American pastor during a time where the nation was dealing with the aftermath of slavery.

Society was entrenched in racism and segregation; however, Seymour rose to the occasion and led a movement that would affect America and the world. White and black attendees alike would gather in his church on Azusa Street to hear the Word of God and be part of the massive revival. This was groundbreaking in its day. The courage, tenacity, and grit of these two leaders can be measured in the impact of Pentecostalism that is still just as relevant today.

At the beginning of the Pentecostal movement in the early 1900s, the Spirit would fall on people and they would be thrown to the floor. Many in that period described it as being overcome by a force where they could only move portions of their body. It was strange and glorious for the churchgoers who had this unusual experience. For some, it would be accompanied by what outsiders described as babbling, or what we know as speaking in tongues.

The core theological beliefs of the Pentecostal movements can be found in the accounts of Acts 2. In his book *Thinking in the Spirit*, Douglas Jacobsen wrote, "Within early Pentecostalism, theology and experience went hand in hand. There is no doubt that experience was a crucial dimension of the early Pentecostal movement, but it was experience guided by theological truth that really mattered."[14] Most of the theological foundation of Pentecostalism came from the Holiness movement that preceded it. This included the doctrine of justification, sanctification, and righteous living. The Holiness movement put major emphasis on living purely and set apart from the world. Its roots were founded in methodism and Quakerism. Early Pentecostalism had these same values, but put major emphasis on feelings or experiences with God. This caused much debating among Pentecostals about how to describe their faith. Theological debate became the norm early on in the movement.[15]

The most notable example of Pentecostal theology comes from Charles Parham and his Bible college in Kansas. Based on his reading of the Bible, Charles came to the conclusion that whenever the baptism of the Holy Spirit was authentically received, it would always result in speaking in tongues. Even though at the time that Charles came to this conclusion in 1900, he had not yet received the baptism of the Spirit, Jacobsen notes that "Parham made this theological doctrine a centerpiece of the curriculum at his school, and he encouraged his students to seek linguistic confirmation of the Spirit's baptism as promised by the biblical text. His students took up the challenge, and soon their hopes were fulfilled."[16] The core of Pentecostal theology focuses on Acts chapter 2. Of course, this is the story of the outpouring of the Spirit. This foundation is important to understand, because from it flows the rest of Pentecostal theology. From that outpouring or baptism of the Spirit comes the gifts of the Spirit. These encompass gifts of prophecy, words of knowledge, healing and the working of miracles. There were many who claimed to be healed and claimed to have experienced miraculous occurrences from the Pentecostal movement.

Furthermore, the Azusa Street revival became the hub of the Pentecostal movement in America and globally. It quickly erupted, bringing about a new phase of Pentecostal history and theology. The revival spread through reporters and attendees who traveled from hundreds or thousands of miles away to experience it. One of the main ways we are able to understand the theological beliefs of the Azusa Street revival is through their mission's semi-monthly newspaper called *The Apostolic Faith*. Clara Lum was one of the leaders of the revival who kept the paper up and running. Jacobsen tells us, "Without that publication, the work of the mission would have been much less well known."[17] William Seymour wanted to be the instructor or teacher of the whole Pentecostal movement. During the years of 1906 to 1908, he extended his teaching mission in large part due to *The Apostolic Faith* newspaper. This paper was mailed out to supporters across the nation and literally around the world. It provided monthly updates of what was happening in the revival, as well as special teaching on the baptism of the Spirit and more.

Pentecostalism brought massive change to the Church. Because of the movement, the baptism of the Holy Spirit with the evidence of speaking in tongues became widely accepted in America and even around the world. In the year 1900, there were at most a handful of Christians who were experiencing this phenomenon, as well as gifts of the Spirit similar to those in the book of Acts. By the turn of the next century, over 600 million Christians identified themselves as Pentecostal or charismatic.[18] That's nearly a quarter of the Christian population. This speaks to the legacy and impact of the Pentecostal movement on the Church at large in the early twentieth century.

Furthermore, Pentecostalism affected society and culture. At the time of the Pentecostal movement in the early 1900s, there was still much dissension between races. Black people weren't seen as equal with White people. They weren't allowed to eat in the same restaurants or sometimes even patronize the same businesses.[19] Black people were made to use separate entrances and were second-class in the eyes of many. In spite of all of this, one of the main leaders of Pentecostalism was a Black man. Although the movement didn't eliminate racism, it did push things in the right direction. It was the first of its kind to have large gatherings of Blacks and Whites in the same building for regular worship gatherings. This pushed the boundaries on colorism and broke societal norms. The Pentecostal movement and later evangelicalism are credited with furthering civil rights in America.

You Are Mantled to Start a Movement

The Azusa Street revival and movement was phenomenal. But that was nothing in comparison to what we are going to experience. We are charting a new course in history. The story is still being written about how God will use you. He may use you to bring social change to some of the issues that are ailing our communities. He may use you to bring clarity and solutions to political challenges that seem immovable. He may use you to bring solutions and answers to the medical industry. He may use you to shift the governmental arena, or arts and entertainment.

The next move of God will impact all spheres, systems, and sectors of the world. It's important that you remove any barrier or limitation on how the Lord may want to show up in and through your life. It doesn't take a whole lot for a move of the Holy Spirit to start. If the Pentecostal movement through Azusa Street could be started by someone who was marginalized, with no social status, no massive wealth, and no extraordinary human ability, then how much more could God cause you to start a move of the Spirit in your neighborhood, city, or community?

Movement is defined as "a series of organized activities working toward a common goal or objective." It is also "an organized effort to promote or attain a purposeful end."[20] Movements may start small, but they are not fully defined as movements until they affect a greater population. Every God-inspired movement carries a supernatural force to help other people, raise the level of thinking, and transform lives. There are certain key factors that every movement carries. As I walk through this list of key factors one by one, you will gain a deeper understanding of how God may use you to put in motion meaningful change in your world. Every movement has:

1. *A catalyst*—According to *Webster*, a *catalyst* is "an agent that provokes or speeds significant change or action."[21] There has to be someone who is used to spark the effort. A catalyst is fearless, bold, and passionate. This individual knows how to push until something begins to manifest.

2. *A core*—God moves through groups and companies of people. In order to reach a common goal or purpose, you need agreement from like-minded people. Matthew 18:20 states, "For where two or three are gathered together in my name, I am there in the midst of them." Greatness is enhanced and multiplied exponentially through people who are willing to come together. One person's skill set will help the others. There is power in uniting as a core.

3. *A cluster*—In Isaiah 65:8 the Lord says, "As the new wine is found in the cluster, and one says, 'Do not destroy it, for a blessing is in it,' so will I do for My servants' sake . . ." The *cluster* here is referring to a bunch of grapes. The strategy for extracting the new wine is found in the bunch, not the single grape. A movement must not only have a group of people who believe in it, but also a cluster of ideas, and a diversity of perspectives melting into one. The anointing from God explodes in the merging of gifts, talents, and skills.

4. *A creed*—A set of key tenets, beliefs, and principles is needed to sustain an initiative. The same is true with any organization or business. In order for a message to have longevity, it has to be fortified by its beliefs. The Bible provides the compass and road map for beliefs that are rooted in truth.

5. *A catapult*—When God determines the appointed time, nothing can stop the launch of what He intends to get done in the earth. As an initiative builds momentum, the wind of God has the ability to give it a thrust forward. This gives that movement increased visibility. This kind of supernatural push can only come from the Holy Spirit. No person or amount of effort can make something into a God-given movement.

MANTLE MOMENT

You are being mantled for a movement! Take some time to think about how God may want to use you to start or become part of a movement in your community or sphere of influence. It doesn't have to be massive to move the hearts of people toward God's agenda. It only takes a willing vessel to become a vehicle for change and transformation. Here are some questions that can help you position yourself to effect change in the lives of others:

1. Are you a catalyst? Are you carrying a message or burden within you to spark change in the lives of others? (Answer yes or no, and why.)
2. Are you called to be part of a core, and have you identified that core group of people? What kinds of people do you desire to be connected to?
3. What are your goals to help positively transform lives and point people to Jesus Christ?
4. What possible movement are you carrying? What kind of initiative do you believe God wants you to start in the earth to bring Him glory?

13

NET-BREAKING ANOINTING

. . . they caught such a large number of fish that their nets began to break. So they signaled their partners in the other boat to come and help them, and they came and filled both boats so full that they began to sink.

Luke 5:6–7 NIV

What God is about to do in your life is going to be groundbreaking. Pause right here and say aloud with me, "This is major!" Heaven is opening over your life, and you are going to be filled with so much wisdom, insight, and revelation that you will be unstoppable.

If you have been connected to my ministry for the last few years, then you may have noticed a shift in how we have been able to serve the Kingdom through various types of gatherings, online marketplace-to-ministry mentorship, and training. Not too long before I began writing this book, our ministry had just come out of facilitating a major gathering in Minneapolis called the Mantle Conference. Maybe you attended or participated with us online. I have been doing conferences for many years, but nothing quite like that one. It was phenomenal. It exceeded our expectations.

You must understand that I never do a conference just to do a conference. You can always pull an event together, but with this one I had a whole other level of knowing and expectancy attached to it.

One year prior to the 2022 Mantle gathering, during the height of the pandemic, the Lord first spoke to me about the conference. The world was at the height of the COVID-19 Delta surge. Everything around us was shut down. There was widespread panic because people were dying from this virus, thousands almost every day. And just as we were covering our church, ministry, and Kingdom partners in prayer, I imagine you were praying, too. In the midst of so much happening, the Lord spoke to me and said, *I want you to host a gathering in April 2022.*

Have you ever experienced a time when God speaks a word to you that seems contrary to the context you are living in, and sometimes out of ignorance you want to say, *God, are You sure?* And that's exactly what I said to the Lord: *God, are You sure You want me to do that? April 2022 is a year from now, and right now we're in the middle of a pandemic. People are going crazy all over the world. I don't even know if they're going to let us gather with that many people in a convention center.*

I know He heard my concern, but He told me to do it anyway.

Trusting the word of the Lord, I gathered my own money and contacted the Minneapolis Convention Center, and I paid for the booking in full. I share this because I want you to know that it was a step of faith for me. I had no understanding in the natural of what things would look like a year from the time the Lord told me to plan the conference. I took a leap of faith, paid for it, and didn't tell anybody that I had locked in the Minneapolis Convention Center. I held it all in confidence for about six months. Then once we came toward the end of 2021, the Lord said to me, *Now is the time to talk about it.*

If you recall in chapter 5, we discussed how there are times when God has called us to something so big that we need to keep it to ourselves and for a time proceed in stealth mode. This was one of those times.

When the conference finally came around, we all knew it was more than a conference; it was revival. It was a move of God, a supernatural outpouring that's still happening, still snowballing to this day. As of now, we are planning the next conference and are expecting more than double the attendance. People are so ready for their next level in God. And the Mantle Conference carries the anointing that will break them through.

The Lord knew that people—after experiencing global panic, sickness, and grief over the virus—would need a divine encounter with Him at the time He set for the conference. So as we approached the end of 2021, He said, *When you get to April 2022, I'm going to give a reprieve. There will be a break where people will be able to gather en masse, and you and all who gather will see the hand of the Lord move.*

The Lord did as He said He would. He cleared the way, and people came—literally thousands of them. We're still reeling from what God did. Every speaker, every person the Lord used at that revival gathering was literally on fire with the word of the Lord for that moment. We not only received solid teaching from the Word, but we also saw the kind of signs, miracles, and wonders we read about in the New Testament break out in our midst. Some of these even came in clusters. So not only did we see the working of miracles; we saw it coupled with gifts of healing.

Even people who watched replays of the Mantle Conference were healed as they watched. We received a testimony of someone who couldn't walk. The person had been in an accident and couldn't even get to the gathering in person, but was healed watching the replay and was able to walk again. A miracle of healing took place right there in this person's life. And we are still getting testimonies. We also learned of others whose tumors dissolved instantly in the presence of the Lord. Everything we experienced confirmed what the Lord had spoken to me more than a year before. God is so powerful. He is a God of healing. Our God is a God of miracles. He gets all the glory for what He did.

What God started then continues to erupt. The words, the teaching, and the miracles we experienced are not stopping because we left the building. The move of God is not stopping because the conference ended. People took what God stirred in them at Mantle back to their churches, homes, and cities. So when I tell you that the Lord is doing something we haven't seen before, something groundbreaking, I am saying this with confidence, with evidence, and with proof. I know we've experienced the birthing of a God-sized vision and dream—something that doesn't make sense in the natural, something so big it's beyond your understanding. All you know is what God spoke to you.

Let me tell you another part of the testimony, and then I'll tell you how it all ties in to this word about the net-breaking anointing God is going to impart into you. It's a word that I know will wreck you, just as it wrecked me. In our planning for the Mantle Conference, we set a budget for the event. But often when carrying out a mission from God, what needs to be taken care of extends beyond the tangible, which in our situation included things like the building, lights, cameras, and so on. As we proceeded with our plans, people would reach out to us and tell us how much they wanted to be at the conference but didn't have the money. The Lord would speak to me about many of their situations and say, *Do it*. I knew what He wanted, so by His direction we took it upon ourselves as a ministry to step out in faith and cover the expenses for many people who wanted to attend Mantle but couldn't afford it. Their costs were an addition to the costs we had already set aside for the speakers we had lined up. We were following God to cover the expenses for random people we had never met before!

What began to happen, obviously, is that the overall cost for the conference increased more and more, until it came to an amount of about $250,000—far above what we had in the original budgeting plans. But on the first night of the conference, the Lord began to move in such a powerful way that we were able to meet that higher budget through the generosity of all who gave. Read that again: In one night, the Lord met the budget for all we had given out over those preceding weeks. He honored all we had done to ensure that He would be able to move in people's lives the way He needed to.

There was such a move of God in that place on the first night of the conference, but He wasn't finished. In one of the day sessions, God began to move on the hearts of people again, so much so that the budget for the *next* year's gathering was covered up to $500,000. He doubled the budget! I know that ministries don't often disclose budgets and what they pay out for certain things. Often as believers, we don't like to talk about money. So I understand that this could be an uncomfortable conversation. But I hope you see through it that what God did wasn't really just about money. What He did was about birthing a movement and a move of God.

This is about when the Lord sees that you're available to help His people and give into the lives of others, and how He will make you a conduit of finances to get help to the right people in their time of need. Right there in that Mantle daytime session—not the general public night service, when attendance is typically highest for conference sessions—people came together and gave. Nobody pulled on them or coerced them to make them do anything. They just gave.

Listen, this level of the manifestation of God's power in our lives is just the beginning. It's bigger than our hosting conferences, planting a church, or launching a business. It's not only about any of those things. God wants to take that dream or vision you have and cause there to be such a breakout of a move of God that your city, church, and community are impacted by what He has placed in you. All you have to do is be available and be faithful to what the Lord tells you to do.

A New Kind of Upgrade Is Coming

As we wrapped up Mantle 2022, I took some time to sit in the presence of God, praying and connecting with Him. Whenever you facilitate or host an event or some other kind of service or gathering, it's important to pull into God after you conclude those things. While I was sitting there, the Lord began to speak to me and tell me what had happened over the couple of weeks before, during, and after the conference. He brought to my remembrance the Scripture passage in Luke 5 when the disciples launched out into the deep, and after toiling all night they brought in such a catch that their nets broke:

> So it was, as the multitude pressed about Him to hear the word of God, that He stood by the Lake of Gennesaret, and saw two boats standing by the lake; but the fishermen had gone from them and were washing their nets. Then He got into one of the boats, which was Simon's, and asked him to put out a little from the land. And He sat down and taught the multitudes from the boat.
>
> When He had stopped speaking, He said to Simon, "Launch out into the deep and let down your nets for a catch."
>
> But Simon answered and said to Him, "Master, we have toiled all night and caught nothing; nevertheless at Your word I will let down the net." And when they had done this, they caught a great number of fish, and their net was breaking.
>
> Luke 5:1–6

I don't know about you, but this passage wrecks me every time I read it. What God said to me about it was—and this is a word for you, too—*What I've brought you into is a net-breaking anointing.*

Now, this was not the first time the Lord had spoken to me along these lines, but there was something about this time that was very different. He said to me, *I want you to look at what happened over the couple of weeks before and after Mantle.*

I understood what He was pointing to. Around the time we were preparing for Mantle, I had also released my second book, *Prophetic Forecast.* The book became an instant bestseller on several lists, including *USA Today.* Between several factors that played out all at once—the excitement around the book, the surging interest in the Mantle Conference, the volume of speaking requests, the incoming emails and messages, and visits to our websites—the number of people wanting to be part of anything we were doing increased exponentially, and our systems began to break. I was in panic because we thought we had prepared. We had pulled the right things together, we had formed new teams, and we had hired companies to help us in areas we couldn't cover. We thought we had things in place. But the Lord used our failed best efforts in handling the overflow to show me a prophetic sign, and it was this: *There are times when you can prepare to the level you are aware of, but when God puts His hand on something, often there is preparation needed beyond what you're capable of at that time.*

As I understand it, the highest level of faith is preparation. Yet what happens when you prepare, but the nets are still breaking? What happens when you prepare, but you are still experiencing things breaking down around you?

To help me answer these questions, the Lord took me again to the passage in Luke. This time, He added more clarity and said that even though we had prepared up to a point, more was needed because *What I'm about to do is going to be so major that your current capacity will not hold what I'm about to give you. Although I've been preparing you and I've been getting you ready, there is another upgrade that has to come, and it will be net breaking.*

Then from Luke 5, the Lord led me to Ephesians 3:20 and said, *I'm going to do above what you can ask or think. When you prepared for the vision I gave you, you prepared at the level you were able to conceive. You prepared for the level you asked Me for, but what you did not anticipate was what I was going to do above what you asked. I'm doing things for you that are above what you can think.*

I'm sharing this testimony with you because I know that what I experienced wasn't only for me. Everything that happens in our lives—every good and perfect gift from the Father—testifies of Him. The overflow we experience is for His glory, so people can see what an awesome God He is, and so they can believe big and believe He has great things in store for them, too.

Even with you, God is using the vision He placed in you to testify of Himself, to release His glory through you. What you currently have won't be able to house or hold what God is about to release in your life. It's going to be major. The Lord says, *What I'm about to do is going to be beyond what you could ask or think.* And there's a supernatural preparation that must take place for your "next," which the Lord has to do. Not for your now, not for where you are, but for what's about to come next.

To put it simply, your nets must break. As He did with me, the Lord will allow your nets to break so that you are convinced you're in need of an upgrade. Your current systems, no matter what you've done to prepare, won't be able to hold what the Lord is about to do. There is a prophetic upgrade coming to your life.

Looking back at Luke 5, we read, ". . . and their net was breaking" (verse 6). Realize that at the beginning of this story, the disciples were coming in from being out all night. One of their tasks between fishing trips was to wash and mend their nets because along with the fish they pulled in, they also pulled in debris and trash that would damage their nets. Repairing their nets was a regular part of their preparation for being ready for the next day's catch.

But when Jesus told them to go out again, the preparation they usually applied was not enough. When they cast their nets this time, the nets started to break because this catch was bigger than what their nets could pull in. There was no anticipating this. They had done all they knew to do, which had worked before with all kinds of catches. But with Jesus there, the whole dynamic had changed. They needed new nets.

Your Nets Are Your Networks

God revealed to me that a net represents our network. It represents the people who have connected with us, those whom we've come into partnership with. Sometimes the current network you are in can only support where you've been, but when the Lord wants to do something greater, you need a different kind of help. He has to send support to your network.

When you experience a net-breaking moment, this is the time when you go through and assess whom God has put in your life and why they are there. When you start to assess the people in your life, you may discover that sometimes leeches have attached themselves to you. They try to leech off your anointing or your name. They have the wrong heart and wrong agenda, and in trying to get something for themselves, they try to pull it off you. To deal with that, you must begin to ask the Lord to show you who the right people are to have in your net, or network, and whom He wants you to join with in this season. Pay attention to the answers God sends to this prayer. There will be times when He will reveal that you're going in a different direction from a certain person who has been in your network for a while. This doesn't necessarily mean something is wrong with that person. It could mean that where God is sending you is simply in a different direction.

In this season of increase and breakthrough, you must assess your net. You have to wash it and remove debris. You'll need to mend it where it has grown old, weak, or frayed. You must counsel with God in order to know and follow His maintenance schedule for your net, because your current network will not hold what God is about to do. Let's look again at Luke 5:6–7: "And when they had done this, they caught a great number of fish, and their net was breaking. So they signaled to their partners in the other boat to come and help them. And they came and filled both the boats, so that they began to sink."

We weren't meant to carry our mega visions from God alone. We were designed to operate in partnership. We were designed to first partner with the Holy Spirit to see a move of God in the earth. Then God has also designed us to partner with others. This is why the enemy fights us so hard with the spirit of competition. It's such a deadly thing. He knows that a house divided against itself cannot stand. He knows how much we would accomplish if we worked in unity. With all God has dreamed for us, we don't have time for competition. We don't have time to be trying to compete with other preachers or the next business down the street. We must come out of the immaturity of competing with our brothers and sisters.

God gave you an assignment, and He gave me an assignment. We're working on the same team. If there are people in your ministry or company who can only feel better by tearing you down and making you look bad, you need to put them out of your network. We're coming into a day and season where we cannot be in partnership with people who don't have the right heart. They will slow you down and hinder the thing God is trying to do. Because when you have the right spirit, are yielded to the Holy Spirit, and are in partnership with the right people, God will do more for you and with you than you could ever imagine. Everybody wins, and everybody will have a seat at the table.

God is raising a people who understand how to celebrate and appreciate what He is doing in someone else's life. He is raising a people who will answer the call to help you pull in the God-sized catch He has led you to. He is raising a people who know what "when you win, I win" means. These kinds of partners know that when you get victory, they have victory. They know that when the Lord does it for you, He just did it for them. They're not jealous, but are secure in their identity in Christ. They don't get upset when they see God using other big gifts or when they see it's someone else's time. They will not feel that because it's your time, they've missed their time. They will not try to ride your coattail and pull anything they can because of their relationship to you. They know that's thievery in the Body of Christ. These are the kinds of people you want in your network, and God may cause your net to break so you can see who is for you and who is not.

Let me also give this caution: Be sure that you are one who has the right heart as well, one who can celebrate other people's wins. The Lord may have you in place to support others in their net-breaking seasons. The Lord is bringing together a people who will win together and be of one accord. Again, in this new season everybody will have a seat at the table.

Covenant Partners on Assignment

Getting back to Luke 5 once more, the last part of verse 7 tells us that these fishermen's partners from another ship came to help them and they filled up both ships, and then both ships began to sink. There was such a large catch that no one ship could take it alone; they had to call for the right partners. I believe that the Lord is about to send the right partners and the right people into your life. He has been doing it for me. He has been sending the right people who have an ear and an understanding on a level I don't.

Likewise, you need to make sure you surround yourself with people who have more wisdom than you, people who are already in the place God is bringing you to. Because they've been there, they will be able to help guide you. Their maturity and genuine investment in your victory and success will be assets to you. You will win with covenant partners like this in your network, and a corporate move of God will extend to everything each of you touches.

Being able to depend on others in this new season is critical for your expansion. God isn't bringing this level of partnership into your life for just a moment, and then after the moment passes the relationship is over. These partnerships are about covenant, because the Kingdom of God works through covenant. God has ordained and designed partnership. He purposefully orchestrated our need for interdependence—I need you, and you need me. Part of being able to build capacity for the great thing God is birthing through you is accepting your need for true covenant partnership.

The Lord is bringing unity among us like we have not seen before, and the right people are about to gather in your life. Don't dismiss them because they may come in a package or in a way you don't expect. Don't dismiss them because they are coming and nobody knows their name. They won't have certain accolades or levels of fame. When the Lord raises up someone as the right covenant connection for you, trust that all of heaven knows their name and hell gets a printout of who they are. Whether they are known in the earth or not isn't important. The Lord has put His stamp of approval on them, and the rest is on God. He has sent them on assignment to help push you, and you are sent on assignment to help push them.

Step into a Place Called *More*

As the Lord imparts to you a net-breaking anointing, you're going to have to go back to your systems and redo everything. You must prepare for greater. With this anointing at work in your life, you're going to have to double the capacity of what you were planning for. You're going to have to manage double the budget you were planning for. The Lord is saying to you that He is going to do more than what you anticipated. He is going to do beyond what you have asked, imagined, or planned. He is saying, *I'm stretching your capacity to handle more.*

More is not just something we receive; more is a place. You can live in a place called *more*, a place called overflow and abundance. I speak over your life right now that you are stepping into a place called *more*. You are stepping into a net-breaking anointing, where you will have to ask for help because the catch will be so big. I decree over your life in the name of Jesus that expansion just hit your entire house, your entire ministry. I decree in the name of Jesus that you're going to have to lengthen your cords and spread out your tents (see Isaiah 54:2). Overflow will become your portion. Everywhere you turn, the blessing of the Lord will overtake you. Doors of opportunity are beginning to open in your life right now. Those challenges you faced in the past—you have now overcome them.

With that net-breaking anointing will also come the anointing to destroy yokes and limitations. You're going to break past barriers that have been in your family line. The limitations you once saw in your life will no longer hold you back. You're going to break past them. They are being broken right now by the power and the authority of Jesus Christ. You are stepping into a place called *more*. You are stepping into overflow, another level, and another facet of your purpose.

MANTLE MOMENT

You are about to experience a net-breaking anointing in your life. As you receive this word of the Lord, understand that you are stepping over into another dimension of what the Lord has called you to do, and it requires greater help.

You have been praying and asking the Lord about how to get the things done that you've been envisioning. It's bigger than your level of expertise and know-how. The Lord says, *I'm sending help to you.* I can hear the Spirit of the Lord say, *Get ready for help to come.*

Not only will you see help in the form of people, but the Lord said to me that there is angelic assistance also coming. You will see and experience the angels of the Lord on assignment in your life, bringing strength to your body, bringing strength to your life. You are going to experience the help of God, and it's coming right now, in Jesus' name.

14

GREATER WORKS

I tell you the truth, anyone who believes in me will do the same works I have done, and even greater works, because I am going to be with the Father.

John 14:12 NLT

Whenever the Lord wants to expand you, He's never expanding you so that you can just look good. As we discovered in the previous chapter, you pay the price for the anointing, and He gets all the glory. And because of the anointing that's on you, He makes you look good. But how you look is not the reason He ordains the expansion.

We must realize that God working in us is about a bigger picture. Sometimes we can be so self-centered, and we must be careful of that demon called narcissism, because it's very easy to have a me-centered gospel. It's this kind of experience where it's all about me and my becoming, or all about me going to a certain place and making it to my next level. These are things we preach, but we have to be careful that we don't take things out of bounds and out of order. We must be careful that we understand the Word of God in the context in which it is given. We cannot have a me-centered type of gospel or a me-centered kind of relationship with the Lord, saying, *Well, if I could just get the blessing . . . if I could just reach my goal . . . if I could just become what God wants me to be.* We must be careful.

I find that the most frustrated people are the ones who are too focused on themselves. If you ever feel as if you're lacking purpose, I challenge you to serve somebody else. If you ever feel as if you're stuck and you don't know what to do, serve somebody else. You don't find your purpose when you're in a glamorous, me-centered type of situation. Your purpose isn't revealed to you when you're on top of the mountain. Your purpose comes to you when you're in the valley. Your purpose comes to you when you're serving somebody else. And serving has to become the greatest part of what we do and who we are. We must pick up a burden for serving again, to the point that we're willing to go beyond our comfort zones and step outside what we're used to in order to impact somebody else's life.

What Is Greatness?

If we call ourselves Christians, but we're never touching or impacting someone else, then we're not a good representation of who Christ is. Christ lived a very different life than the picture we paint of Him. You may remember the picture of Jesus that used to appear in printed Bibles. That depiction of Him looks very different from what Scripture describes. Revelation 1:14–15 describes Him as having hair like wool as white as snow, eyes like flames of fire, and feet like burnished bronze. Anytime you look at a snapshot of who people have painted Jesus to be, you get a different kind of Jesus. The Jesus we read about in Scripture was the kind of person walking the earth who made sure He found Himself serving. Although He was God wrapped in flesh, He was the very one washing the feet of His disciples. He wasn't the one having His briefcase carried. He wasn't the one with the entourage. He wasn't the one saying, "I need you to make sure you get me some water." He was the very one who said, in the midst of all of the glory He possessed, "Let me wash your feet. Let me teach you how to serve" (see Matthew 26:14–39; Luke 22:24–27; John 13:1–17).

Jesus said, "If any man wants to be the greatest, let him become a servant" (my paraphrase; see Matthew 20:26). We cannot be great until we become small, until we reduce ourselves. I know this goes against the prevailing messages being promoted in some places. Love yourself, pursue yourself, even date yourself are some of the themes telling us to consider ourselves more than we consider others. But Jesus is teaching us to become smaller so He can become greater. Let your flesh submit to His will. Let your dreams die so His vision can come alive. This is a message that we don't teach, but that Jesus was teaching His disciples. He said, in effect, "If any of you even thinks you are the greatest, you need to realize that the greatest becomes the servant of everybody."

If you find somebody great in the Kingdom, know that you've found a person who is willing to serve—and do it without capturing it on video and showing people that he or she is feeding the homeless. A servant of all can pay for somebody's groceries in the grocery store and not write a post on social media about it.

If you want to find somebody who is great in the Kingdom, I'll show you somebody who has rolled up his or her sleeves and is standing in the trenches, laying down his or her life to pick up the burden of Christ. That's a servant, and these are the great ones in the eyes of God.

Are You a Servant?

You may be surprised at how many negative responses you get if you ask the people you go to church with, "Are you a servant?" Nobody wants to serve. This is why churches have problems recruiting people to volunteer to fill basic needs. Nobody wants to serve without some kind of payment or favor—you do something for me, platform me, or do this or do that.

I do understand that people are worthy of honor, and we can aspire for more, or for promotion. But many times, people don't want to serve without receiving a clear personal benefit. When asked to serve, they may think things like, *Can you show me something that's a benefit if I do?* Even when they simply show up and don't serve, they think, *What will I get for showing up to church, God? What kind of blessing will You give me this week because I came? I didn't miss a Sunday at all last year. Where are my blessings?*

Then when things go bad in our lives, we start calling out our record, and that's never something the Bible tells us to do. The Bible shows us that when things go bad, we need to call out God's record and remind Him of who He is (see Isaiah 43:26). My record doesn't matter. Neither does yours. You can go to church every Sunday, never missing a beat. You can read Scripture every day and pray three times a day. But when it comes down to it, God's record is the only record that counts. When you're caught between a rock and a hard place, your perfect attendance isn't going to deliver you. According to Isaiah 64:6, our righteousness—the right things we do—can never measure up. Jesus' blood and righteousness are what cover us. It's His perfect record that God sees.

Our real service to God should be based out of our love for Him. Everything else that happens as a result of what we've done to serve Him is just icing on the cake. Real service leads us to say and think, *God, I'm going to be there for You, to worship You, and to serve You, because I love You. It's part of who I am.*

Real Ministry Isn't What We Think It Is

I believe God is trying to bring the Church back to a place of serving Him for real. I remember this particular group of people I mentored some time ago, and one of the first things the Holy Spirit led me to guide them through was a stripping away of pride. He encouraged me to help them learn what real ministry is. In so many ways, we've substituted what we see on Instagram and Facebook posts for real ministry. We've substituted what we see on a platform for real ministry. But real ministry finds us in the most uncommon places of our lives. Real ministry shows up right when you're there, minding your own business. Real ministry shows up when you're sitting there at the restaurant, trying to eat your own food, and the Lord nudges you about serving the person sitting at the table beside you. That's real ministry.

Real ministry can't be put in a box. Real ministry isn't something you can put on your schedule. When real ministry shows up, it finds you at the place where you would never expect it to. It finds you there when you're just trying to get your work done on your job, or you're just trying to meet your deadline, or you're just trying to meet whatever quota you have. The Lord speaks during times like these, saying, *You see that person over there? He [or she] is going through depression and needs prayer.*

Real ministry is serving even when your body and mind don't feel like it. It's showing up when everything in you is saying, *God, I really don't have time for this*, or *God, this is going to mess up my plan. It's going to mess up my schedule. It's going to mess up everything.*

When we're thinking about being a great minister, pastor, prophet, or even marketplace leader, the Lord will require some of us to go through a "backside of the desert" kind of experience like He led Moses through. In Exodus chapters 2 and 3, Moses ran into the wilderness and ended up tending someone else's sheep (his future father-in-law's flock). The Lord will require others of us to go through the school of hard knocks. Real ministry is not as easy as some of us think.

You may have watched other people go through the process of launching into a ministry, a career, or a new business, and it seemed as though immediately they were spotlighted or promoted. While I was ministering in the States not too long ago, someone said to me, "It seemed as if you just popped up overnight." Someone else said, "Yes, we had just heard of you, and then your name was just everywhere."

"Well, that's the misconception," I replied. "I've traveled to over 35 nations and have been serving in full-time itinerate ministry for over fifteen years, while nobody knew my name."

The key is that nobody has to know who you are. When we start substituting our name for God's name, then that's a problem because our goal is not to make our name great. Our goal is to make His name great. If you can minister throughout the nations and people still don't know who you are, that's a good thing, not a bad thing. It means you've been exalting His name and not your own.

There's No Cookie-Cutter Greatness

In the Kingdom, there's no cookie-cutter greatness. We've made ministry into a business, and not the message and service it's supposed to be about. Ministry has become something to package. You need to have the right branding, the right look, and the right stuff to attract the right people. Satellite churches are the new franchises, and leaders are able to offer custom-built worship centers: "I can put this kind of church in your city," or "I can put that kind of church up for you."

Church has become this cookie-cutter, McDonald's model where we install a popular worship leader, upload a good crowd, and stream the right points in the sermon. But I'm reminded of how the Church started. The early churches were so different from each other that the apostle Paul had to write different letters to the different groups of believers, addressing different situations because the needs of one church in one area were completely different from the needs of another church in another area. If I tried to infuse the DNA of a church from one area into a church in another area, then I could be missing the assignment of that region and territory. We can't reduce the *ecclesia* to a popular praise-and-worship leader and to cookie-cutter sermon bullet points.

What happened to being called to pastor? What happened to being called to pioneer? Becoming a pastor cannot be reduced to feeling like a pastor, finding a mentor, and then you're ready. Often, people are promoting others into positions where the hounds of hell are waiting to rip them apart because they haven't been called. They haven't been sanctioned by God and aren't ready for the assignment. We cannot just make you something you are not.

What happened to movements being birthed in prayer, without ego? Nobody wants to serve anymore, and this is why our churches struggle. Real ministry is about serving somebody else.

Your Serving Is Never in Vain

Self-gratification has us asking, "What are you going to do for me? How are you going to help me?" But that's not what the Bible tells us. The Bible says that our mission is to serve somebody else. The more we serve, the more God begins to exchange our service and humility for grace and favor (see Proverbs 3:34; Matthew 23:12; James 4:6). You can never sow something in the spirit that you won't get back in the natural.

Don't think that for all these years you've been serving your spouse, boss, or leader who hasn't done anything for you, God hasn't noticed. You can't sow anything in the spirit and not get it back in the natural. God remembers and says, *I am your God. I will repay. I'll restore the years you've served. I'll restore the years you were broken down.*

God is not a liar. You may have served under difficult circumstances for fifteen years and, even though you've given from your heart and out of love for God, it can still feel discouraging not to see promotion or appreciation. You may wonder, *Does anyone see what this has been like? Is there breakthrough for me? Is there more?*

We desire to receive love and gratitude, and there's nothing wrong with that. When people are grateful for what we have done, it helps us know that what we gave was well received. But we must be careful whom we put first. Receiving praise from people and pleasing people cannot be our initial or central motive. It should always be about God. When our hearts are in the right place, it's His pleasure to return to us what we have sown.

So yes, you may have sown and served for fifteen years, but if God has you there, don't grow weary in well-doing (see Galatians 6:9). It could be in that sixteenth year that a tsunami of blessing and increase hits your life. You can give for twenty years, and it can seem as though you're getting nothing back in return. But you've been doing well. You've given everything you have. Don't you let the devil trick you out of your next anointing or blessing that's about to hit you. You may suffer for a while, but the day is coming when your suffering is about to transfer into blessing and promotion.

Your serving is never in vain. Don't let anybody make you think that you can serve for years in a place God has positioned you and nothing will come of it. As you fed the hungry, healed the sick, sheltered the homeless, and counseled and prayed for those in need of direction and wisdom, God saw it all. And when you're in need, the same God who helped them through your service is the same God who will help you.

What the Bible says is true—it is better to give than to receive (see Acts 20:35). Receiving is good, but giving is so much better. Receiving is good, but serving is better. You'll find joy when you serve. You get an anointing when you serve. You get peace when you serve. Serving is greatness in God's eyes.

You may have come to this chapter thinking that I was going to prophesy to you about caravans of money being transferred to you as you are being platformed on large stages around the world. While this may be part of what God has planned for you—I don't know your unique circumstances—greatness starts here, with humility and service. I do know that you may be sowing in tears today, but the day is coming where you will reap in joy (see Psalm 126:5).

You may be giving in anguish today, but the day is coming where God begins to count up the cost, and the angel of God comes and tallies up everything you've been doing. And God says this: *I am not a man, that I should lie. Neither am I a son of man, that I should repent. I will not owe you anything. If I said it, I will do it* (see Numbers 23:19).

Your Mantle Is More than Money

You may have heaps of heavenly treasures waiting on you with interest because of how you've served in the trenches when nobody knew you or paid you a dime. I can't tell you the number of initiatives I've taken on because the Lord said *Do it* when nobody paid me a dime.

I remember there was one service I had just finished preaching at where somebody came up and asked me, "How much money did you get for doing that service?"

I didn't go into details with the person, but the truth is that I had taken on the assignment knowing it was unpaid. I got zero dollars for the service. As a matter of fact, I went in the hole doing that service because I sowed an offering into the organization.

While we are so focused on numbers or on being seen and acknowledged, we can miss our mantle. We can miss the anointing, which will actually carry us farther than a dollar amount will. The favor of God sitting on your life will take you to a place where not even money can open the door. God looks at you and says, *That's my son . . . That's my daughter . . . I'm looking out for them. They've been serving faithfully. They've been serving well. There is no good thing I will withhold from them.*

You Want Greater?

We want the greater works, but we don't want our posture to change. We want the greater works so we can get the glory. But look at what the Bible says in John 14:12–14:

> Most assuredly, I say to you, he who believes in Me, the works that I do he will do also; and greater works than these he will do, because I go to My Father. And whatever you ask in My name, that I will do, that the Father may be glorified in the Son. If you ask anything in My name, I will do it.

What Jesus doesn't say here, but I can sense His implication, is that *I'm not going to do it because you're so blessed and highly favored.* He didn't say, *I'm going to do it because I just love you so much,* although He does. He didn't say, *I'm going to do it because you were obedient,* even though that's one of the ingredients. What He said, in effect, was, *Whatever you ask in My name, I'll do it so that My Father in heaven might be glorified in the Son.*

God is about to do something so great through you, in you, and with you, in order that the Father in heaven will be glorified through the Son. *The reason I'm about to pour My blessing out on you*, God says, *is because I desire the glory*. You are about to see expansion come in a way that you have never seen before because God will be glorified through it.

Be careful, however, of glory thieves. Be careful of people who want to take the glory for themselves. Be careful of people who say, "I healed that person," "I opened that up for them," and "I did . . . [this or that]." Be careful of being a glory thief yourself, because the greater works are not for you to bring glory to yourself. God said, *I want to use you*. Remember that the greater works He said you'd do are to glorify God the Father and to make His name great.

God called and chose you, and He led you through all you went through so He could use your life to bring glory to His name, not so glory could come to your name. The Lord will allow you to go through some of the hardest trials so that you're processed to the point where you don't want His glory for yourself. When we still want our name in lights, we're not ready for greater works. When we're still looking to validate ourselves through the works, we're not ready for them.

Going back to the story about the group of people who had asked me to mentor them and who needed to go through "humility training," I'm reminded of what the Lord led me to tell them. It was this: "The Lord says you're going to have to get acquainted with real ministry. In this next season of your life, for however many years, you will serve and preach the Gospel, and nobody is going to care about your name."

I realize that this is not the kind of mentorship everyone can take, but we must really question ourselves: *Are we really after God? Do we want Him for real?* Because what we will find when the Lord really begins to put His mind in our minds is that the way we've been taught and the way we've been thinking are out of alignment with what He wants and desires.

What would God say if He came right now to inspect our fruit? What would He say if He came right now to inspect what we've done, what our character is, how we carry out any kind of assign-ment we have? What would He say about our fruit, about what we carry? That's the important thing we need to focus on. *God, how am I serving? Am I serving well, or am I doing something for my own gratification? Am I serving You, or am I doing this for my own attention?*

The motive, the why, is always important. Yes, God said we're going to do greater works, but the why is important.

Greater Is Going to Cost You

To accomplish His earthly assignment and to activate it so it would be carried out long after He transitioned out of His fleshly form, Jesus recruited what seemed to be a random group of people to follow Him and learn the ways of the Kingdom. This sounds exciting from our context, but can you really imag-ine it?

The Bible says that the disciples dropped their lucrative busi-nesses to follow Jesus. He was not well-known then as the Son of God. He was just some man, but I imagine Jesus must have been such a man of influence. Because no one can just walk up to somebody and say, "Come and follow Me," and have the per-son do it! Not many people can drop a business that's making them money and follow after God. But the Spirit of God must have borne witness to the disciples-to-be that if they trusted this man, they would carry something so much greater than a natural legacy. They were about to pick up the assignment of God in the earth.

We find the same thing with Elijah and Elisha, where Elijah threw his mantle on Elisha, and then Elisha began to follow Elijah. As they were leaving, Elisha asked, "Can I please go say good-bye to my father and mother?" (see 1 Kings 19:20–21). And Elijah replied, in so many words, "You aren't ready to come with me. You're still trying to make peace with your past."

You aren't ready to pick up the assignment of God until you're willing to walk away from your past without any kind of worry. It's not until we can forget those things that are behind us that we can press forward to the mark of the high calling and to those things that are ahead. As the apostle Paul put it, "Brethren, I do not count myself to have apprehended; but one thing I do, forgetting those things which are behind and reaching forward to those things which are ahead, I press toward the goal for the prize of the upward call of God in Christ Jesus" (Philippians 3:13–14).

Many people are unwilling to let go of their own in order to pick up something greater. What about you? The Lord has something greater for you. What are you willing to give up? What are you willing to let go? If you want the anointing, you're going to have to sacrifice. There's something God will want in exchange. Greater is going to cost you something.

I know it's not popular to teach this way. Preachers don't tell you that you'll have to sacrifice something. "Jesus paid it all," they'll say. That's true, He did. But that was for your salvation. The anointing is going to cost you. Your salvation is free, but for the anointing, there's a price.

It's Not Personal; It's Purpose

If you're wondering about the cost of the anointing, ask Joseph. His father stitched an amazing coat of many colors for him, a colorful mantle representing every piece of life experience that he himself, Jacob, had gone through (see Genesis 37). Jacob spent time putting his energy, his breath, and his life into the coat. He saw that somewhere in the spirit, there would come a day where Joseph would need wisdom and Jacob wouldn't be there to give it to him. So he stitched his son a mantle.

The Lord always gives you the mantle before you're ready to carry it. This is exactly what He did for Joseph. God used Joseph's father to give him a coat of many colors. This was like a mantle. Jacob put this coat of many colors on his son, and Joseph's brothers were looking at him and saying, "He thinks he's special because he has that coat. He thinks he's all that. Look at him."

And Joseph was special. Jacob made this coat for one of his sons and not the others. I know we have this idea about God that He's fair, but the Bible doesn't say God is fair. He is not. God is just. There's a difference. Because if we wanted fair, we wouldn't be sitting here right now. If we wanted fair, out of all the messes we've made, we would have been dead somewhere a long time ago.

God is not fair, but He is just, which means He will balance out the scales for you. He is the God who will put a coat on one and not on the other. Ask Joseph's father. God said, "Jacob I have loved, but Esau I have hated" (Malachi 1:2–3; cf. Romans 9:13). What He was saying, in essence, was that *I put My hand on Jacob, but I rejected Esau because of purpose.* Jacob put that coat on Joseph, but the other sons seemed to feel as though they were rejected. Yet it was about purpose. It wasn't personal.

You have to understand that what you must go through for the anointing isn't personal. It may feel as though it is. If you take your life experience personally, you will be walking around angry at everybody, including God. This is why God must take you through a process of refinement and maturity. When we understand God's love for us and that His plan for our lives is good, the difficulties become easier to overcome. We see God's hand in each of those moments and understand His purpose for leading us through them because they were part of a bigger picture. We come out understanding how true it is that God turns those trying times around for our good. We come out delivered from pride into a place of total surrender.

I'm telling you that if you can take it, you will pay the price for the anointing. And by the time you get through all of that, you will be ready for where God is taking you.

Think Big

Position matters, but position is determined based on purpose. Of the twelve men Jesus called to follow Him, He pulled three in closer based on the purpose in the assignment they had. He was more transparent with them. Then He also imparted into the whole Twelve at a level He didn't do with the masses. He began to teach and train this group of men and they became apostles, or sent ones. In other words, they were commissioned by heaven to carry out an assignment.

Then there were the seventy in Luke 10:1, whom Jesus sent out two by two. These are the ones He commissioned and poured into, saying, "You will do greater works, greater miracles than what you saw Me do." He was telling them (my paraphrase), "You're going to have greater impact than what I had. You will see more people come to the Father than what I saw in My ministry."

We talk about the miracles of old, and all we saw God do in our churches when we were growing up, and the harvest of people who came in. But God is saying, *Church, you are about to do greater.* It's always a father's intention to see his children to do more than he did. With God, it's not about your physical height or stature; it's about the spiritual works you will do that will be greater.

So if God has commissioned us for greater, why are we doing less? Where are the greater works? In John 14:12, Jesus said, "Most assuredly, I say to you, he who believes in Me, the works that I do he will do also; and greater works than these he will do, because I go to My Father." When I began to research the word *greater* in this verse, the meaning blew me away. As I talked about in chapter 1, it's the Greek word *megas*, where we get our English word *mega*. What the Lord told me as He revealed His context for this word in our lives today is, *What I'm about to place on you is so big, it's mega. What I'm about to give you is so great, you're going to be carrying mega. Mega is going to be so deep in your spirit that you will wear it as your spiritual mantle.*

It's possible that the people around you may be telling you to keep things small in your life. Yes, you might reduce yourself, but what you're carrying is going to be mega. Something on you is about to be big. God gave you the big vision because you are about to do something greater than what we've seen and read about in Scripture.

You may be thinking small, yet God said, *I'm giving you mega.* What you're going after is too small. God needs you to awaken to your new mega reality. He is giving you mega so that He can get the glory. This is why Ephesians 3:20 says that God gives you a bigger thing than what you asked for. You were going for something that was so small, but God is going to expand you.

What God wants to do in your life is so big that your mind can't handle it. You have to ask the Holy Spirit to help you catch up with what God is about to release. You're about to push over into a mega breakthrough. You're about to step into a mega expansion. You're about to walk into mega wealth. You're about to see a mega harvest of souls.

You've paid the price. Don't you dare let the enemy whisper into your mind and tell you that what God is doing is small, when God has said it's big. Your reach is about to be mega. Your impact is about to be mega. Your assignment is not small. God has said your assignment is mega. If you could only see in the spirit what God has shown me. God must get the glory for it.

A Worldwide Anointing

When God told Moses to gather seventy elders in Numbers 11:16–17, He said, "Go and get seventy. Bring them in, because I want to do something I've never done before" (my paraphrase).

So Moses called the seventy together, and the Bible says that God took a portion of the Spirit on Moses and put it over into the seventy. Why did God need seventy? Because what was in Moses was so big that it was mega. It couldn't just go into one person. Moses needed help carrying what God had placed within him.

Looking back at Luke 10, we see that Jesus also chose seventy. The same way God put the Spirit that was on Moses into the seventy in the Old Testament, Jesus began to breathe life into the seventy He had called, and they stepped out and began to do greater works. What's significant about the number seventy? Why did both Moses and Jesus gather seventy? The number seventy goes all the way back to Genesis 10, where the lineage of the first descendants of Adam and Eve were named. The number of descendants adds up to seventy, and they are the origin for every nation now represented on the earth. So what God was saying, in essence, is, *Give Me one elder, one disciple from every nation represented on the earth, that they may go out and do greater work to testify to the world My glory and power.*

Understand that when you see the number seventy, it's a number that represents "worldwide" or "international." It's a number representing mega. It signifies to us that what God is going to do in this season is bigger than ethnicity and race. It's bigger than the cities and communities we come from. It's bigger than the countries we live in.

The mega power of God is about to come on you to impact somebody else who doesn't look like you or sound like you. Mega is coming upon you so that you will fulfill the assignment of the prophecy God has released concerning your life. Because of the magnitude of what you carry, people will look at you for the rest of your life and say, "How did you get that? How did that happen for you?"

Your mega is not just going to be one season. God has called you to a life of greater works to glorify your Father in heaven.

The blessing of mega is going to sit on you because God wants to bring glory to His name through you. All you need to do is move you and your ego out of the way.

When Greater Hits Your Life

When your life is charged with the purpose of fulfilling God's mega vision, people are going to ask you, "How did it happen? How did you get it? How did you do it?" They will be baffled at the speed with which you rise up and take up your position. The things you'll be able to accomplish in record time because you wear a mantle for greater things will be numerous.

People will say to you, "I tried to do that very thing, but it didn't work for me. How did it work for you?" Things that took others twenty or thirty years to do, you will do in a fraction of the time. The questions will pour in: "How did you reach that many souls?" "How did you feed that many people?" "How did you impact that?"

You're going to answer, "It's because God has mantled me for greatness. I'm carrying an anointing called *mega*."

I'm telling you that the anointing, vision, or assignment you carry is greater than what you know. It's greater than what you see. Don't be fooled by where you are right now. The Lord is going to stretch out your capacity. He is going to lengthen your tent pegs and enlarge your borders. His hand is on you, and this is the reason the enemy can't stand you. The enemy has tried his best to take you out throughout your life because he knows there's something greater in you. He's been trying to fight it your whole life. But your purpose is so much bigger, and God has protected you.

For you, mega is not a season or a chapter. Mega is your life. I decree that from this day forward, the purpose of God will manifest in you in such a powerful way. You will serve in a mega way. You will go above what you did in the past. You will reach more people than you've reached before. The Lord is placing the influence on you necessary for the assignment.

The word *mega* also means "a loud voice." What I sense coming through this mega mantle is the Lord amplifying your voice. You are about to reach into places with your voice, your words, where you couldn't reach before. When you speak, you will reach people and they will hear you in ways they couldn't hear you before.

With the release of mega on your life, don't despise the days of small beginnings, as we talked about in chapter 9, because it starts off small. It's not apparent at first that what you carry is something that will shake nations. Be patient. Remain faithful.

When the Lord called me to the nations, my ministry was housed in a storefront church, in a little room that held fewer than one hundred people. I studied and prepared my messages in a little box of an office, and I wouldn't even take a salary. As a matter of fact, I still don't. But it was at this time that the word of the Lord came to me. He said, *Don't you dare look at your surroundings. Don't you look at where you are, because I have placed something in you that's bigger than where you are.*

Little did I know that from that storefront, the Lord would send me to 35 nations. But that small room that held fewer than one hundred is where it all started. That was eleven years prior to the writing of this book. Since then, the Lord has performed all that He said He would, and then some. Although I am blessed and grateful, I know that none of it is about me. Every open door and every level of expansion and increase is a vehicle to bring glory to God's name. He will do the same through you.

Not too long ago, I sat in a meeting with a major international company. They had their top people there, and we were discussing some event our ministry had put on. They said to me, "We don't understand how you did it. Do you have a team? Was there a company you hired?"

I said, "Absolutely not."

They said, "Well, what was your strategy? What marketing plan did you use?"

I said, "I didn't have a plan or strategy. All I had was God. It was no company, and no money. It was just God who did it."

They looked at me and said, "But you didn't have . . ."

I said, "No. It was just God."

Your testimonies will sound just like this, where all you'll be able to say is, "It was just God."

I want you to know that God rewards. He brings mega. He brings mega release and expansion, and we are in the time of it right now. This is just the beginning. If you haven't seen it, don't get discouraged. Take this word and let it strengthen your faith because you are about to be overtaken with the blessing and power of God. Mega is your portion, in Jesus' name.

MANTLE MOMENT

God is mantling you for greatness! But you are going to have to "Think Bigger" than the way you've currently been thinking. Ephesians 3:20 states, "Now to Him who is able to do exceedingly abundantly above all that we ask or think, according to the power that works in us." Your thinking is directly connected to what God wants to do in and through you. For this "Think Bigger" exercise, I want you to make a list of five ideas that you have. They could be ideas for missions, ministry, business, or life. Write down your realistic goals. After you've written them, go back and raise the bar. Think of ways you can expand and stretch them to be even more impactful. This exercise will help you put your reliance on God and not on your own human ability. As you practice thinking bigger, your mind will expand for the next level God is bringing you to.

15

CATCH THE MANTLE

Then Joshua said to the people, "Consecrate yourselves, for tomorrow the LORD will do wonders among you."

Joshua 3:5 ESV

There is a changing of the guard. God is bringing down some and raising up others. Mantles have been released in the earth, but they are hovering in the realm of the spirit because no one has picked them up.

What I saw in the spirit were voids, gaping holes where the mantles of giants, spiritual leaders, and generals who have passed on or who have become of a certain age were hovering there, unclaimed and unoccupied. These mantles have been left there not because God doesn't want them operative, not because God cannot perform, and not because of a shortage on God's part. They hover there because the right people haven't stepped into position to carry the mantles into the future.

However, there are those of us whom the Lord has been preparing. Of this number, there are still some who have not sacrificed to the level God has been challenging them to. There is a clarion call going out into the earth. We must step into position because there are mantles waiting to be filled.

Like you, I have studied revivals and moves of the Spirit in the past. Like you, I have been there. Maybe you grew up in an era where you saw miracles being performed, God bringing souls in, drunk people coming into the Church and the Lord sobering them up. If you are like me, you remember seeing people high on drugs getting delivered instantly, never to return to that lifestyle again. We've seen amazing moves of God throughout our lifetimes, but the Lord began to say to me, *There's more that I want to do.* So in this season and the era we are in, we can either be high off a past move and be stuck in a past thing, or we can put on the mantle and be positioned and propelled toward something more.

That No Flesh Should Glory

Not long ago, I was praying and the Lord said to me, *I WANT to demonstrate My glory. I WANT to show Myself strong to My people.* His words caught me off guard because there have been times in the past when I have prayed and sought Him, saying, *Lord, show Your glory. Lord, demonstrate Your power.* Yet during this particular time of prayer, I couldn't even get to my request because the Holy Spirit was already there, saying, *I WANT to show up. I WANT to demonstrate. I WANT to move in power.*

We are now in this place where the Holy Spirit wants to do more; He is just looking for people who are available. They don't have to have a special title. They don't need ordination papers. They don't have to have the approval of everybody around them. The only prerequisite is that they believe.

If you are a believer and you avail yourself to God, He is saying to you, *I want to use you in this day. There is a work I want to do through you, but I'm waiting for you. Are you willing to pick up the mantle?*

The word *mantle* comes from the Hebrew word *'aderet.*[1] One of the definitions means to shroud the flesh or cover the flesh. This word gives the picture of God placing a mantle on an individual so that as the person ministers, no flesh is able to glory in God's sight (see 1 Corinthians 1:27–29). In other words, no flesh is seen because there is a covering over it.

When God places a mantle on you, He covers up your deficiency. That means that He covers you because in your own self, you are weak. In your own self, you are not enough. It is only through Jesus Christ that you become enough. So when He places a mantle over you, He is saying, *I'm stepping into the place where you are weak, the place where you come up short. I'm going to move supernaturally.* And so, as we discuss mantles, I believe the Lord is now challenging us to catch the mantles that have been hovering, pick them up, and wear them to cover our flesh—our weaknesses and deficiencies—so that the Holy Spirit Himself can move.

The Lord is about to pull you into times of consecration. It may be your practice to fast and pray as you come into a new year, or for other reasons. I believe that the Holy Spirit is giving us another push, and that in this season of more, of expansion and growth, we will be led into waves of consecration. As it says in Joshua 3:5 (ESV), "Consecrate yourselves, for tomorrow the LORD will do wonders among you." We know from our discussion back in chapter 5 that consecration is the doorway to accessing the supernatural wonders of God.

Consider the net-breaking anointing God is placing upon you and how, through it, the Lord is telling you that you will have to go back to the drawing board and get ready to expand your vision. You will have to make more room, because revival is coming and you will see a harvest.

Jesus said it this way in John 4:35: "Do you not say, 'There are still four months and then comes the harvest'? Behold, I say to you, lift up your eyes and look at the fields, for they are already white for harvest!" In other words, He is saying, *Understand and begin to declare that the harvest is here right now.* We are coming into a period of revival and harvest. We will see the hand of the Lord begin to move and break out in our lives in unusual ways.

Even as you read these words, prophesy them over yourself. This word from the Lord is about to catch fire in you. As you pick up this word, you are going to see the Spirit of the Lord moving in unusual ways—ways you won't be able to put into words.

The Mantle Will Cost You Everything

In this time of harvest, there will be unexplained miracles. For example, the Lord told me that we need to get ready to see a supernatural move in computer systems. I call these "cyber miracles," where the Lord begins to move in systems. In this case, He will move in computer systems to cancel out debts. I gave this word to a man in my church one Sunday. I told him that I saw hospital bills of his that were piled up, but that the Lord had said He was about to cancel this man's debt. Literally within a week, the man gave the testimony that he was awakened from a nap by a phone call telling him that his debt was canceled. The Lord canceled thousands of dollars of debt that this man had been praying about and believing God to move on. These are the kinds of things we will see the Lord do.

However, the voids and vacancies in the spirit—these gaping holes God showed me—need to be filled. The Lord is calling for more laborers, more people who are willing to surrender and avail themselves to Him enough to pick up the mantle and carry on what He desires to do now and into the future. I am reminded of the words of Kathryn Kuhlman, where she began to declare and say to the people that it cost her everything to step out and do what God had called her to do. It cost her literally everything.[2]

This is a sobering word, one that I believe the Lord is challenging us with. He wants us to know that if we want to see the next dimension and level of anointing He will pour out on the Church, it will cost us everything. If we want to see miracles like the unexplained debt-cancelation testimony I shared become commonplace, we must wholly surrender everything to God. We will have to die to our flesh, ourselves, our egos, and our selfish agendas and ambition.

Come Back to the Altar

The Lord has placed an amazing call on your life. You have an anointing on you, but He is waiting for the next level of your surrender. He is waiting for you to give up that thing you've been holding on to. The minute you let it go is the moment that God says, *Okay, now I can fill you up because you've been emptied out of yourself.*

The Lord is challenging us to die to ourselves. He is challenging us to stop chasing after microphones, front seats, and the approval and praise of mankind, and come back to the altar, the place of consecration where we meet Him for real. It's at the altar that we have true encounters with Jesus Christ. I'm not talking about a meeting in a church or a meeting with a preacher. I'm not talking about hearing a message that gets you excited. I'm talking about a place where you have a real encounter with the Holy Spirit and He revolutionizes your life. When you encounter God for real, you can't leave and be the same way you were.

I feel a pull in the spirit to prophesy this to you now: As you arise to the challenge and begin to surrender, the Lord hears you saying, *Yes, Lord, I will pay the price to carry the mantle.* He says this to you now: *As you begin to pay that price, you will see a quick work in your life. I will raise you up quickly.*

It will not take years, because we don't have that kind of time with what's going on in the world. The Lord is raising up people now. There is a move going on now. There is a Kingdom movement happening in the earth right now. There is a quick work in you that must take place so you will be in place to help facilitate and steward what God is releasing.

The hand of the Lord will be upon you in a new way, and people around you may not understand. They may get upset and may even be jealous, because they'll wonder how you could get to this next level so fast. They know where you came from. They know your past, but this is when you tell them that it's all God's doing. This is when you tell them it wasn't you. Let them know that the hand of the Lord is on your life. You've been mantled for greatness. You're not bragging. You're not being arrogant. This is your identity.

You are being called out from among them, and the mantle of greatness is being placed upon you—covering your limitations, weaknesses, and deficiencies so that the name of the Lord will be magnified and known throughout the earth. While some people are stuck on seeing you as you, God is seeing you as He is, and He is using your gifts to the level of your faith and surrender to build and advance His Kingdom. It's not about you. This harvest season, this season of expanse, is all about God.

A Remnant Is Rising

I've been concerned about the divide that exists between this generation and the one before it. If you are part of the previous generation of church folk, as I am, then you know how we grew up in an era when you could walk on the grounds of a church and before you even got into the building, people would be healed and delivered in the parking lot. My parents were pastors, and I watched the move of God break out many times where there were weeks and months of revival. People wouldn't even go to the hospitals. They would drive to church, believing, *If you could just get me to the house of God, I know He'll heal my body.* And we watched God do that very thing.

There was such a high level of faith and expectancy about the moves of God during those times. But there is such a divide right now between what we saw in the past and where we are today. We are now in an era in the Body of Christ where people choose performance over the power of God. There is a form of godliness, but a denial of God's power (see 2 Timothy 3:5). Yet I believe that the Lord is raising up a remnant. There are some hungry and desperate people to whom the Lord is saying, *I'm calling you. I'm choosing you to pick up the mantle and begin to push forward in the Spirit. I'm calling you to begin to surrender, die to your flesh, and begin to allow the Holy Spirit to use you as a vehicle for My glory.*

There is a glory coming so strong that we will no longer be talking about what God did in the past. We will be proclaiming what He is doing *now*—things we have never seen before. Miracles and salvation stories we have never witnessed before will happen in front of our eyes.

I am already hearing reports of such things. At times, I minister over in the Middle East, as well as in other countries, and I've heard reports of people there who didn't know anything about Jesus. They are receiving visions where Jesus reveals Himself to them, and they are being saved through those encounters.

But God is also calling for laborers. While He can do it all by Himself, He desires to work in partnership with us to redeem the world and expand the Kingdom. We have a covenant and commission from God to extend His gift of salvation to all who will receive it. Through the witness of our testimony, whether our mandate is within the four walls of the church or in the marketplace, we demonstrate the immense power of God, to which people will be drawn. The question is, *Will we pick up the mantle?*

We are in a season and era where the gaping holes that have been there in the Body of Christ, where we have seen powerlessness, are going to be filled. A remnant—a breed of believers—is rising to fill them. We are that remnant, if we are willing to pay the price. When we do, I believe we are going to go after God with everything we have.

Hold the Baton

The time is now for you to catch the mantle. It's not too late. It doesn't matter if you have gone years feeling that you missed God. Your time to say yes to Him is coming back around again. You may be reading this in your sixtieth year of life. I'm here to tell you that you haven't missed the call. There may have been some delays, but your time is coming back around. The Lord is aying to you, *Catch the mantle. Pick it up. Pick up My assignment for your life. Pick it up, and begin to run with it. Do it now. It's not too late.*

You may be reading this and feeling very young and inexperienced. What I see is that the Lord is marrying together the Moses and the Joshua generations. No longer will there be a stigma on age. The remnant will not be the ones saying either "they're too old" or "move aside; you're too young." Both generations—young and old—will run together in the spirit. Both old and young will carry the mantle to accomplish great things in the name of God.

We have seen a divide in the Body of Christ in America, but it's coming to an end. We're not competing one generation against another. We have an assignment, a legacy assignment to complete together. And it's not just a passing of the baton, because we've seen emphasis on this idea that some are getting too old and they just need to pass the baton. Perhaps. But have you ever watched a relay race? Maybe you've run track, so you may know that there's a point when the person running begins to pass the baton, and for a short time both runners hold the baton together as they run. As I talked about earlier, that moment provides the picture for the season and era we're in now. The Lord says, *You're going to be running together on this assignment, old and young generations. Catch the mantle. There will be a move of the Spirit among generations.*

MANTLE MOMENT

Catch your mantle! Reading this, you feel something stirring deep in your spirit. There is a rumbling of greatness locked inside you that needs to be released. You know the words the Lord has spoken to you in the night hour. His words lit a fire in you that spoke to the desires you hold tightly in your heart. You can't deny that you were created for more.

Maybe it's an idea for a healing ministry that has been locked up within your spirit, that you never fully walked in. The Lord says that the time is now. I hear it in the Spirit.

Maybe you have a strong deliverance ministry inside you, but you've been battling yourself. The Lord is about to break that limiting mindset off you, and you're about to move in deliverance ministry in a major way.

You may be an evangelist, but you feel as though you've been stuck. Maybe you've been sitting there with whatever it is that God has uniquely designed for you to do, and you haven't stepped out yet. I'm telling you by the Spirit of the Lord, there is a thrust coming upon you right now. I can feel it in the Spirit. Your gifts are about to awaken, and the anointing that has been placed in your bloodline is about to wake up in you. It doesn't matter if your mama didn't do it, or your grandfather didn't do what the Lord placed in him to do. You are about to do it for your generation.

It's time for you to catch your mantle. It's time for you to run with the thing that the Lord has placed in your spirit. You don't need to wait. You don't need to delay anymore. Do what the Lord has placed in your spirit. You are mantled for greatness!

NOTES

Chapter 1 Small Is the New Big

1. BlueLetterBible.org, s.v. "megas" (Strong's G3173), https://www.blueletterbible.org/lexicon/g3173/kjv/tr/0-1/.

2. Aaron Earls, "Small Churches Continue Growing—but in Number, not Size," *Lifeway Research*, October 20, 2021, https://research.lifeway.com/2021/10/20/small-churches-continue-growing-but-in-number-not-size/.

3. Karl Vaters, "About Pivot," *Pivot* (blog), *Christianity Today*, https://www.christianitytoday.com/karl-vaters/about/about.html.

4. "Average number of people per family in the United States from 1960 to 2022," *Statista*, https://www.statista.com/statistics/183657/average-size-of-a-family-in-the-us/.

Chapter 2 You, the Big Idea!

1. John J. Parsons, "Hebrew Names of God: *Elohim*—Creator and Judge," Hebrew4Christians Ministries online, https://www.hebrew4christians.com/Names_of_G-d/Elohim/elohim.html#loaded.

2. *Oxford Learner's Dictionaries*, s.v. "complex," Oxford University Press, https://www.oxfordlearnersdictionaries.com/us/definition/english/complex_1?q=complex.

3. Ibid., s.v. "innovate," https://www.oxfordlearnersdictionaries.com/us/definition/english/innovate?q=innovate\.

4. Ibid., s.v. "idea," https://www.oxfordlearnersdictionaries.com/us/definition/english/idea?q=idea.

5. Ibid., s.v. "mantle," https://www.oxfordlearnersdictionaries.com/us/definition/english/mantle_1?q=mantle.

Chapter 3 Help! I'm Carrying Something Bigger Than Me

1. *Collins English Dictionary*, s.v. "surrender," https://www.collinsdiction ary.com/us/dictionary/english/surrender.
2. *Dictionary.com*, s.v. "cycle," https://www.dictionary.com/browse/cycle.

Chapter 5 Pivot

1. *Merriam-Webster Dictionary*, s.v. "pivot," https://www.merriam-webster .com/dictionary/pivot.
2. Bible Study Tools, s.v. "Qadash" (Strong's 6942), https://www.bible studytools.com/lexicons/hebrew/kjv/qadash.html.

Chapter 6 The Ceiling Is Breaking

1. Mahatma Gandhi, quoted at Goodreads.com, https://www.goodreads .com/quotes/50584-your-beliefs-become-your-thoughts-your-thoughts-be come-your-words.

Chapter 7 Mantled to Break Curses

1. Judith L. Fridovich-Keil, "Epigenetics," *Britannica* online, last updated December 6, 2022, https://www.britannica.com/science/epigenetics.
2. BBC Future, "Can the legacy of trauma be passed down the genera- tions?", BBC online, https://www.bbc.com/future/article/20190326-what-is -epigenetics#:~:text=A%202015%20study%20found%20that,involved%20 in%20the%20stress%20response.
3. BlueLetterBible.org, s.v. "patér" (Strong's G3962), https://www.blueletter bible.org/lexicon/g3962/kjv/tr/0-1/.
4. *Oxford Learner's Dictionaries*, s.v. "submission," Oxford University Press, https://www.oxfordlearnersdictionaries.com/us/definition/american _english/submission#:~:text=submission-,noun,one%20of%20resistance %2C%20not%20submission.

Chapter 8 Mantled for Miracles

1. Blue Letter Bible, s.v. "energēma" (Strong's G1755), https://www.blueletter bible.org/lexicon/g1755/kjv/tr/0-1/.
2. Blue Letter Bible, s.v. "energeō" (Strong's G1754), https://www.blueletter bible.org/lexicon/g1754/kjv/tr/0-1/.
3. Blue Letter Bible, s.v. "energēs" (Strong's G1756), https://www.blueletter bible.org/lexicon/g1756/kjv/tr/0-1/.
4. Bible Hub, s.v. "1411.dunamis," https://biblehub.com/greek/1411.htm.
5. Ibid.

Chapter 9 The Law of Accumulation

1. *Wikipedia*, s.v. "Henryk Grossman," last modified January 12, 2023, https://en.wikipedia.org/wiki/Henryk_Grossman.

2. William Ballard, "How to Apply the 'Law of Accumulation' to Your Business and Your Life," Entrepreneur.com, September 16, 2014, https://www .entrepreneur.com/business-news/how-to-apply-the-law-of-accumulation-to -your-business-and/237363.

3. David took refuge in the cave of Adullam after he escaped Achish, king of Gath, and while he was still on the run from the murderous King Saul (see 1 Samuel 21:10–22:2).

Chapter 11 Passing the Baton

1. Bible Study Tools, s.v. "Genea" (Strong's 1074), https://www.biblestudy tools.com/lexicons/greek/kjv/genea.html.

2. Ibid., s.v. "Genos" (Strong's 1085), https://www.biblestudytools.com /lexicons/greek/kjv/genos.html.

3. Ibid., s.v. "Eklektos" (Strong's 1588), https://www.biblestudytools.com /lexicons/greek/kjv/eklektos.html.

4. Ibid., s.v. "Thesauros" (Strong's 2344), https://www.biblestudytools .com/lexicons/greek/kjv/thesauros.html.

5. Ibid., s.v. "Kleronomeo" (Strong's 2816), https://www.biblestudytools .com/lexicons/greek/kjv/kleronomeo.html.

6. Ibid., s.v. "Metron" (Strong's 3358), https://www.biblestudytools.com /lexicons/greek/kjv/metron.html.

7. *Oxford Learner's Dictionaries*, s.v. "influence," Oxford University Press, https://www.oxfordlearnersdictionaries.com/us/definition/english/influence _1?q=influence.

8. Bible Study Tools, s.v. "Tsalach" (Strong's 6743), https://www.biblestudy tools.com/lexicons/hebrew/kjv/tsalach.html.

Chapter 12 Mantled for a Movement

1. J. Gordon Melton, "Pentecostalism," *Britannica* online, last updated November 18, 2022, https://www.britannica.com/topic/Pentecostalism.

2. C. Douglas Weaver, and Rady Roldán-Figueroa, eds., *Exploring Christian Heritage: A Reader in History and Theology*, 2nd ed. (Waco, Tex.: Baylor University Press, 2018), 200.

3. Mark A. Noll, *Turning Points: Decisive Moments in the History of Christianity*, 3rd ed. (Grand Rapids: Baker Academic, 2012), 310.

4. Robeck Bartleman, *How Pentecost Came to Los Angeles: The Story Behind the Azusa Street Revival* (Ashland, Mo.: Gospel Publishing House, 2017), 7.

5. Ibid., 10.

6. Ibid., 12.

7. Ibid., 13.

8. Schonborn Hocken, *Azusa, Rome, and Zion: Pentecostal Faith, Catholic Reform, and Jewish Roots* (Eugene, Oreg.: Wipf and Stock Publishers, 2016), 3.

9. Cecil Robeck, "The Azusa Street Mission and Historic Black Churches: Two Worlds in Conflict in Los Angeles' African American Community," in Amos Yong, and Estrelda Y. Alexander, eds., *Afro-Pentecostalism: Black Pentecostal and Charismatic Christianity in History and Culture* (New York: New York University Press, 2011), 25.

10. Ibid.

11. Noll, *Turning Points*, 311.

12. Sarah Parham, *The Life of Charles F. Parham, Founder of the Apostolic Faith Movement* (New York: Garland Publishing, 1985), 22.

13. See Gardiner H. Shattuck Jr., "Seymour, William Joseph," in Edward L. Queen, Steven R. Prothero II, and Gardiner H. Shattuck Jr., eds., *Encyclopedia of American Religious History*, 4th ed. (New York: Facts On File, 2018).

14. Douglas Jacobsen, *Thinking in the Spirit: Theologies of the Early Pentecostal Movement* (Bloomington: Indiana University Press, 2003), 3.

15. Ibid.

16. Ibid., 4.

17. Ibid., 59.

18. Noll, *Turning Points*, 310.

19. Robeck, *The Azusa Street Mission*, 25.

20. *Merriam-Webster Dictionary*, s.v. "movement," https://www.merriam-webster.com/dictionary/movement.

21. Ibid., s.v. "catalyst," https://www.merriam-webster.com/dictionary/catalyst.

Chapter 15 Catch the Mantle

1. BlueLetterBible.org, s.v. " 'aderet" (Strong's H155), https://www.blueletterbible.org/lexicon/h155/kjv/wlc/0-1/.

2. Kathryn Kuhlman, "It Will Cost You Everything," Women of Purpose and Destiny, YouTube.com, streamed on July 20, 2018, YouTube video, https://www.youtube.com/watch?v=wkuvXqVz-xc.

Joshua Giles is an apostle, prophet, and sought-after conference speaker. He has traveled to more than 35 nations in Africa, Europe, and the Middle East. He is the lead pastor and founder of Kingdom Embassy Worship Center in Minneapolis, Minnesota, and founder of Joshua Giles Ministries and the Mantle Network. Joshua reaches out internationally through apostolic centers, prophetic schools, and training modules, and he has been consulted by government officials, dignitaries, and national leaders seeking prophetic counsel.

Further, Joshua is a media influencer and popular podcaster, with over a quarter of a million downloads and subscribers. His social media show *Global Prophetic Forecast* averaged up to eighty thousand viewers weekly, and his weekly videos on his YouTube channel and other social platforms do the same. He has been featured on national TV and media outlets, including the Christian Broadcasting Network (CBN), It's Supernatural! Network (ISN), and *Charisma* magazine.

Joshua has a double bachelor's degree in business management and psychology, and a master's degree in theological studies. He has devoted his time to helping Christian entrepreneurs, training leaders, and empowering believers. He has a great desire to help others succeed in what God has called them to do. More than anything, it is his ultimate desire to do the will of God for his life. To learn more about Joshua and his ministry, visit:

www.joshuagiles.com
Facebook.com/ProphetJoshuaGiles
Instagram@joshuagilesglobal